## The Experience of
# GOD

# The Experience of

# GOD

## ICONS OF THE MYSTERY

# Raimon Panikkar

*Translated by Joseph Cunneen*

**Fortress Press**
**Minneapolis**

THE EXPERIENCE OF GOD
Icons of the Mystery

Cover image: Uyuni Salt Lake © Frans Lemmens / Iconica / Getty Images
Cover design: Laurie Ingram
Book design: Josh Messner

Interior illustrations: Original lithographs by Richard Kathmann. All images © Richard Kathmann 2002–2005 and provided by Corridor Press, Otego, New York, corridorpress.com.

*Library of Congress Cataloging-in-Publication Data*
Panikkar, Raimundo, 1918-
  [Icons del misterio. English]
  The experience of God : icons of the mystery / Raimon Panikkar; translated from French by Joseph Cunneen.
    p. cm.
  ISBN 0-8006-3825-5 (alk. paper)
  1. God. 2. Experience (Religion) 3. Mysticism. I. Title.
  BT103.P3613 2006
  231.7—dc22
                                                2005036753

Manufactured in the U.S.A.

# CONTENTS

5

# 4  Privileged places of the experience of God  — 89

# PROLOGUE

One needs a great deal of boldness, ingenuity, and innocence to publish a book today on the experience of God, especially one without any footnotes. It grew out of a week of conferences I gave a few years ago on this theme for theology professors at the Benedictine monastery of Silos. Since the audience was composed almost entirely of Christians, the atmosphere of these pages and its language is Christian, although comprehensible, I believe, to those who do not belong to that religious tradition. In my defense is the fact that I also have written a book of a thousand pages, which has appeared in Italian, on "the Vedic experience."

When we speak of our supreme experience, the very word *God* becomes problematic, although we cannot avoid employing one word or another.

I hasten to note, moreover, that in spite of its ambiguity, the experience is a literal impossibility. There is no possible experience of God, at least in the monotheistic sense of the word. We too often have imprisoned God—the academic expression would be "tried to comprehend God"—in terms of our contingency and our condition as creatures.

Neither is there an experience of God for itself (subjective genitive). There cannot be a genitive in God, for that would add nothing to what God is. Even the verb *to be* is inappropriate.

Nevertheless, the phrase keeps recurring, in tradition and in this book. It has served as a conventional reference to designate the ultimate, the infinite, the mysterious, the unknown, the unseizable. Our title is hence a paradox, a paradox that we defend because the only language possible in this case is paradoxical and oxymoronic. This may relativize both our language and our very conception of the divine.

It is to all this that this book makes allusion.

# 1

# SPEAKING OF GOD

The experience of humanity, expressed in innumerable traditions, both oral and written, has called God by numerous names. Almost unanimously, it has named and understood God as name or as symbol, not as concept.

The origin of the word God is Sanskrit: Dyau, day, suggests brilliance, the light, divinity (like theos in Greek). Light makes it possible to see and light gives life. It is not at all by chance that the sun is accepted universally, including by Roman Catholic Christianity, as one of the divine symbols.

There is a politics of terminology. In our day, the different means of communication give words a considerable power. There are numerous ways of understanding the word God, and no one has a monopoly on its meaning. I often have asked myself if a moratorium on such a word would not be healthy. But, not having the power to propose such a thing, we too will make use of the name God, drawing from it the best possible advantage, encouraged by the ancestral wisdom of humanity. This little book is nothing but a meditation on the meaning this frequently (and badly) used word still can have. If some readers are allergic to it, I would ask them to change it and try to see if, by chance, we are not referring to a common preoccupation.

In the nine propositions that follow, we do not pretend to say anything about God's self, but simply situate the point at which our discourse on the subject of God can have meaning and fruitfulness for those hoping to live a fuller and freer life. The question about God is not first a question about a Being but rather a question about reality. If the traditional "question about God" is no longer the central question of existence, then there is no longer a question about God. It has been displaced in favor of whatever problem has taken its place. Furthermore, we are not asking here if Someone or Something with such or such attributes exists. We instead are posing questions about the meaning of life, the destiny of the earth, and whether there is a necessity for a foundation. We ask ourselves simply: What is the ultimate question for each of us? For what reasons would we dare not to ask such a question?

## Requires a preliminary interior silence

Every discipline starts from presuppositions that permit the discipline to approach its own sphere. In the same way one has need of sophisticated laboratories and complicated mathematics to detect an electron, the appropriate method for speaking about God calls for a purity of heart that knows how to listen to the voice of transcendence (divine) in immanence (human).

Without purity of heart, not only can one not "see" God, but it is equally impossible to have any idea of what is involved in doing so. Without the silence of the intellect and the will, without the silence of the senses, without the openness of what some call "the third eye" (spoken of not only by Tibetans but also by the disciples of Richard of Saint Victor), it is not possible to approach the sphere in which the word *God* can have a meaning. According to Richard of Saint Victor, there exist three eyes: *the occulus carnis, the occulus rationis, and the occulus fidei* (the eye of the body, the eye of reason, and the eye of faith). The "third eye" is the organ of the faculty that distinguishes us from other living beings by giving us access to a reality that transcends, without denying, that which captures the intelligence and the senses.

## Has its own style

Discourse about God is radically different from every other discourse on every other subject because God is not an object. Were God to be spoken of as object, God would become nothing more than an idol.

The word *God* makes reference to a field of research and teaching radically different from all others. Take physics, for example. It is not that God is mysterious and physics is not. The concepts of physics—energy, force, mass, number—are as mysterious as the word *God*. But in physics, even though in many ways we do not know what physical reality is, we nevertheless devise or affirm parameters that permit us to measure regularity or to formulate possible laws in regard to the functioning of physical reality. Such an operation is not possible in regard to God. There are no adequate parameters that would permit us to speak of the "functioning" of that reality we call *God*.

Discourse about God is unique and cannot be compared to any other human language. It is irreducible to any other discourse.

## Involves our whole being

This is not simply a discourse of feeling, of reason, of the body, of science, of sociology, nor even of academic philosophy or theology. No instrument can localize God. Discourse about God is not an elitist specialization.

We do not need to meditate to open ourselves to the mystery of God. To speak, or feel, or be conscious of God, we certainly need the mediation of language, feeling, and consciousness. But we do not need a particular language, a predetermined feeling, or the content of a special consciousness. The only possible mediation is our own being, our naked existence, our very entity between God and nothingness.

The *Book of the Twenty-Four Philosophers,* so often cited and highly esteemed by Christian scholastics, declares in proposition 4: *Deus est oppositio ad nihil mediatione entis,* "God is the opposition to nothingness through the mediation of being." There is no other mediation except ourselves. We have no need of mediation, because this ultimate that we are, our being, is precisely mediation. "The creature is the mediation (the mediator) between God and nothingness," Thomas Aquinas has written. In brief, *esse est co-esse,* "to be is to be with." Our being is being with God. There is no absolute monism.

The human experience from all times has tried always to express a mystery that is found both at the origin and the end of all that we are, without excluding any of it. God, if God "is," cannot be found either on the right or on the left, neither on high nor below, whatever meaning we give to those words. To pretend to situate God on our side, against others, is quite simply a blasphemy.

## Regards God alone

God is not the monopoly of any human tradition, neither of those who call themselves theists nor of those who are called, wrongly, believers—wrongly, since everyone believes in one thing or another. Nor is God the "object" of any kind of thought. A discourse desiring to imprison God in any kind of ideology would be sectarian.

In other words, Christians are able to speak in the name of Christ, Buddhists can invoke Buddha, Marxists Marx, democrats Justice and Liberty, philosophers Truth, scientists Exactitude, Muslims the message of Muhammad. And each of these human groups can believe itself the interpreter of a conviction that comes from God or from reality itself, whether we call it faith, evidence, reason, common sense, or anything else. But if the name of God is to play a part in all that, it ought to be as a symbol of another order, a symbol that serves to uproot the absolutism of every human activity, a symbol that expresses the contingency of all human enterprises, thus a symbol that makes impossible every totalitarianism of whatever type there may be. "Not only is God not exterior to the world but he is absolutely interior to it," Zubiri said. So interior to the world is God that we cannot separate God from the world metaphysically, nor divide God politically, nor compartmentalize God socially.

## Needs the mediation of a belief

It is not possible to speak without the mediation of language nor to utilize language without expressing some kind of belief, although discourse about God never should be identified with one particular belief. There is a "transcendent relationship" between the God of whom we speak and what is said of him. Western traditions have called it *mysterion,* mystery, which does not mean enigma or the unknown. The Names of God have no link with God, and each denomination of the mystery represents an aspect of that mystery, of which we cannot say whether it is one or multiple.

Each religion is a differentiated system of mediations of this mystery. Every language is particular and linked to a culture. Each language depends on a concrete context that gives it meaning, while at the same time limiting it. So it is necessary to take into account the fundamental inadequacy of every expression. In this light, for each religion to defend its formulations is not a scandal, on condition that it respect the others and acknowledge that each mediation is only a mediatization, as it were. This does not prevent the fact that we can, and should, argue about the greater or lesser adequacy of the expressions employed, without forgetting, however, that the interpretation of every text requires the knowledge of its context and the intuition of its pretext.

The traditional "proofs of the existence of God" offered by Christian scholasticism, for example, only prove the non-irrationality of the divine existence to those who already believe in God. Otherwise, how would they be able to recognize that the proof "proves" what they are seeking? It is obvious that what is proved depends on the *probans*—that which proves—and that the *probans* is a great deal stronger and more powerful than what is proved.

## Regards symbol and not concept

God cannot be the *object* of a knowledge or of any belief whatsoever. The word *God* is a symbol that both reveals and veils itself in the very symbol of which we speak. Every symbol is such because it is, and not because it is interpreted within an objective context of knowledge. There is no possible hermeneutic of the symbol, because its proper interpretation is found in itself. The symbol is *sym-bole* ("to throw together" in Greek) when it establishes a relationship with us—that is, when we recognize it as such. A symbol that does not speak immediately to the one who perceives it ceases to be a symbol. People can teach us to read symbols, but as long as we do not understand directly what we are reading, the symbol is a dead letter.

Unlike concepts, which are univocal, at least in intention, symbols bear several meanings. The symbol is eminently relative, not in the sense of relativism, but in the sense of relativity, of the relation between a subject and an object. A symbol is something to be contemplated and does not pretend to be either universal or conceptual. The symbol is concrete and immediate—that is, without intermediary between subject and object. It is at once objective and subjective; constituitively, it implies relation. The symbol symbolizes; therefore, it establishes a relationship with what is symbolized in it and not with any "thing" else.

Were language only an instrument to designate objects or transmit a simple piece of information, then discourse about God would not be possible. Nevertheless, people do not speak only to transmit information but also because they have a constitutive need to speak—that is, to live fully by participating through the word with a universe that is, in its turn, inseparable from the *logos*, the word.

## Includes several meanings

Discourse about God, in terms of its very constitution, has numerous meanings. There cannot be one primary meaning, *primum analogatum*, since there cannot be some metaculture on the basis of which such a discourse would be developed. There exist many concepts of God, but none of them "comprehends" him. A super-concept or a conceptual common denominator would not resolve the problem, because it would eliminate from the scene what are precisely the richest and most suggestive diversities and would turn God into an abstraction. God is not a mere formality.

We ought to accept the fact that multiple religious traditions exist, that we cannot make measurements or comparisons among them, and that the "universal God" we might be tempted to postulate as the common denominator of all these traditions certainly would not be the actual God of any real tradition. God is unique, hence incomparable, and the same is true of every experience of God. There is no prior space, both neutral and common, that would permit us to establish comparisons.

To pretend to limit, define, or comprehend God is in itself a contradictory effort, since its achievement would be a creation of the mind, a creature. To wish to discover something more vast and more encompassing than God is a distortion of thought—although we obviously are able to compare different ideas of divinity.

## Does not exhaust the divine

Pluralism is inherent to the human condition and prevents us from speaking of God by starting from a single perspective or a unique principle of intelligibility. The very word *God* is not necessary. Every claim to reduce the symbol *God* to what we understand by that symbol not only would destroy the symbol but also would cut our links with all those peoples and cultures that do not feel the necessity of that symbol. The pretension of offering a unified scheme of intelligibility on the universal level is a remnant of cultural colonialism. To universalize our own perspective is an unjustified extrapolation. The very possibility of a "global perspective" is surely a contradiction in itself.

Philosophers and theologians certainly would be able to nuance the two preceding affirmations, but perhaps the solution would emerge more easily if we cut the Gordian knot of a universal theory about God and rediscovered the divine as a dimension of, or pluralism (not plurality) within, an aspect of reality itself.

## Leads back to a new silence

A purely transcendent God would become a superfluous and even perverse hypothesis, even apart from the internal contradiction of all discourse about him: How is one to speak of that which is purely transcendent? Such a hypothesis would obscure the divine immanence while simultaneously destroying human transcendence. The divine mystery is ineffable and no discourse describes it.

It is the nature of human experience to know that human experience is limited, not only as a linear segment limited by the future but also by its composition, by the very foundation that is given to it. Without love and without knowledge, without corporeality and without temporality, this experience is not possible. *God* is the word, quite audible for some but less so for others, that gives us, in breaking the silence of being, the opportunity to find it again. We are the ex-istence or "standing out" of a *sistence* or "standing" that permits us to spread out (in time) and extend (in space). Our existence coheres with the whole universe in which we insist on living, when we persist in our quest and resist the cowardice of frivolity, subsisting precisely in that mystery that many call God and others prefer not to name. Silence is the matrix of every authentic word. It is out of the primordial silence that the *logos* emerges, writes Saint Irenaeus. Silence is the place where time and eternity embrace.

# 2

# THE EXPERIENCE OF GOD

## The silence of life

Often the immediate character of what is *urgent* distracts our attention from what is *important*. Fundamentally, it is a question of the tension between practice and theory. If the urgent is not important, we throw ourselves into a counterproductive practice; in that case, the "urgent" can wait and is not worth the trouble. If the important is not urgent, we sink into an erroneous theory; the important then becomes nothing but a simple abstraction. I would define prudence as the harmonious union of the urgent (a function of time) and the important (a function of weight). The art of knowing how to combine the urgent and the important is a characteristic of wisdom, one of the conditions for living well.

If we were able to forget for a moment that we are professors, builders, business managers, and so on, if we were able to forget that we are Christians, and even human beings, we would facilitate thereby an openness to an awareness of reality for which we can be spokespersons. For this purpose we ought to divest ourselves, we ought to relieve ourselves of the entire ensemble of attributes that limit us, although they correspond to our personality, and that often asphyxiate us if we identify ourselves exclusively with them.

The silence of life is not necessarily identical with a life of silence, like the silent life of the desert monks. The life of silence is important and necessary to realize our objectives, to plan our actions or develop our relations, but it is not the same as silence of life. The silence of life is that art of making silent the activities of life that are not life itself in order to reach the pure experience of life.

We frequently identify life itself with the activities of life. We identify our being with our feelings, our desires, our will, with everything that we do and everything that we have. We instrumentalize our life while forgetting that it is an end in itself. Plunged into the activities of life, we lose the faculty of listening, and we alienate ourselves from our very source: Silence, God.

Silence appears at the moment when we position ourselves at the very source of being; the source of being is not being but the *source* of being—being is already on this side of the curtain. That prior place, the one that is earlier, the place of beginning, is the silence of life. To say this in Christian terms: "I have come in order that you may have life, life in abundance" (John 10:10). The entry into silence is not a flight from the world, a dichotomy between the essential and the relative. It is the discovery that the essential is essential uniquely because I speak starting from the relative. And the relative is relative only because I discover that a relationship exists that permits me to be in silence when beginning with the essential.

It is not a matter of taking importance away from the activities of life. We certainly cannot live without eating, any more than without thinking, without feeling, without loving. We have spoken of the third eye, that third organ or faculty that opens us to a dimension of reality transcending the knowledge we can acquire through the intellect and the senses. Without a silence of the intellect and the senses, this faculty would remain atrophied, and, as a consequence, life—the experience of life, the life anterior to its expression in different activities, life in its depths—would escape us. Under such conditions the link with the latent world remains hidden; participation in cosmic plenitude, as well as with the gods and demons, is not taken into account. In this way our lives, deprived of their source, become impoverished, sad, and mediocre. To overcome this destitution we have recourse to a multitude of things that sweeten it, enrich it, and give it meaning, importance, and dignity. We identify ourselves with this multitude of things; we drown ourselves in this constant activity. Then we forget that the flower, the lilies of the field, the bird, do more "for the glory of God" than all our efforts, our impatience, and our careers. We have a nostalgia for another life when we do not live life. Jesus said something about eternal life, which he promises us immediately. Simeon the New Theologian even says, "The one who does not live eternal life here below will not enjoy it later on."

## Constituents of the experience

The experience of God includes four distinct but inseparable moments:

• The pure experience, the instant of pure life, of immediate experience.

• The memory of that moment, which permits us to speak of it, but which already is no longer pure experience, since it passes through the mediation of recollection. Memory cannot be separated from experience but it should not be confused with it.

• The interpretation we develop of this, which leads us to describe it as painful, sensitive, spiritual, loving, the experience of Being, of God, of Beauty, and so on. The interpretation we give of the experience is linked intimately to the experience itself, to memory, and obviously to our language.

• Its reception in the cultural world that we have not created but which has been given to us and which bestows on experience a special resonance. Every experience is inscribed in a cultural environment outside of which it is not necessarily of further value.

This four-dimensional experience, which is always personal, can communicate itself by contagion (resonance), love, assimilation, education, and other means, including subjective participation. It cannot be communicated by a simple extrapolation of objective concepts, as if it were a question of a formal entity. In consequence, it is not possible to have a universal science of human experiences, and hence the inevitability of intercultural discourse.

These experiences of ultimate mystery are the great experiences that have forged the different cultures of humanity and their history. Indisputably, the reception of an experience in the framework of a given tradition conditions the interpretation that is made of this experience. The great traditions emerge generally from extraordinary experiences most often received as revelations. Through memory, the interpretation of this experience survives and is transmitted, an interpretation which, in its turn, is conditioned by the culture in which it has been received.

Take, for example, the experience of Jesus, which provoked among his contemporaries strong memories. These experiences were recorded in documents and have led to the interpretations the first Christian communities developed out of this memory. The reception progressively made from those memories constitutes tradition. Its reception, conservation, transmission, deformation, and augmentation give form to religion and serve to explain the richness of an experience that has created a whole civilization. The phenomenon is very complex, for it is not only a question of the experience of Jesus but of the numerous other experiences (of Christ) that Christians have believed they have had afterward. In consequence, the living tradition is more than a simple exegesis of a past experience, a fact that a certain kind of theology seems to have forgotten. Theology is not archaeology.

There is no theology without language, and language already is culture. Religion gives culture its ultimate content, and culture gives religion its very language. It follows from this that the relation between religion and culture is constitutive for both, and that consequently we ought to recognize that:

• there is no religion without culture and no culture without religion.

• the experience of God is not the monopoly of any religious system, of whatever denomination, nor of any church, nor, basically, of any culture.

• we need the mediation of language and language is already a cultural phenomenon.

As a consequence, all our ideas about God, like our memory and the interpretation that we elaborate on the basis of experience, utilize the mediation of a concept, a belief, and a religion. We cannot separate them, but we can distinguish between them. Some time ago I suggested a formula that might be useful to recall here: E=e.m.i.r.

What we call experience ($E$) is a combination of personal experience, which is ineffable, unique each time and foreign to repetition ($e$), conveyed by our memory ($m$), modeled by our imagination ($i$), and conditioned by its reception ($r$) in the cultural context of our time.

I have used the word "combination" in the chemical sense, that is: $E$ is not equal to $e + m + i + r$, for the identity of the separate constituents is distinct from its entity in the combination. Water is not $H + O$ nor even $H_2 + 0$ but $H_20$, in which the elements have lost their separate identity.

In consequence, we cannot, for example, affirm without further precision (as is too often the case) that the mystical experience ($e$) is or is not the same in all religions, for we have access only to $E$.

It is in this context that we must situate the problem of the encounter with other religious traditions. It is necessary to arrive at what I have called an "ecumenical ecumenism." One of the most urgent tasks of the world today is the establishment of bridges between the different religions. That does not mean that, because of love of tolerance and ecumenism, we ought to dissolve that which constitutes the specificity of each religion, but it does mean that this specificity should express itself in its complete integrity.

I have spoken of this in a book with an ambiguous title, *The Unknown Christ of Hinduism*. There I suggest that the "unknown Christ of Hinduism" is not the Christ known to Christians and unknown by Hindus. I assert that there are other aspects of this same Christic mystery that Christians do not know, and that Hindus know under another name; Christians call this mystery Christ, although under aspects that are unknown to them. The formula of John, "Christ is the *alpha* and the *omega*," implies that Christ is *alpha, beta, gamma, delta,* all the way to *omega*: he is all. Everything is found in this Christ who is prior to Abraham, of whom Christians know a name and understand an aspect; but they do not understand the totality of the mystery. The historic phenomenon of Jesus is thus an epiphenomenon of the mystery of Christ, which does not mean that he is neither real nor central. While for Western culture the historical fact is taken as the fundamental character of reality, for Eastern culture it is only an epiphenomenon.

## Faith, acts of faith, and belief

In order to explain the experience of God, which we are attempting to approach, it is appropriate to distinguish between faith, the act of faith, and belief.

The word *faith* has many meanings. We have faith in something, we give testimony of our faith, and so on. And to increase its ambiguity, the action expressed by the substantive *faith* is spread out in at least three verbs: to have confidence, to put it in the hands of, and to believe. The title of this chapter must be understood in its most profound, most philosophical meaning, in relation to the problem about God.

Faith is a constitutive element of being human. Every person, by virtue of the fact of being human, has faith, in the same way that every person, by virtue of the fact of being human, possesses reason and feelings. One person may have a more obtuse and another a keener reason, one a more lively sensibility and another a more dull one. In the same way, everyone has faith, whether cultivated or neglected, whether or not he or she is conscious of it.

By faith I mean the capacity of opening to something "more," a capacity not given us either by the senses or the intelligence. This openness to a more could be called an openness to transcendence. Through faith, people are capable of transcending themselves, of growing, of opening themselves to a more; they are capable of making a leap toward what is neither justified by their senses nor proved by their reason.

Faith is inscribed in the heart, as the word *credo* indicates; the same thing is seen in Sanskrit with the word *shraddhâ* (to give the heart).

Faith is that capacity, faculty, or supplementary possibility (that would be the simplest word) of transcendence (the most philosophical word) of God (the most theological word). *Capax dei,* the scholastics would say: a person is capable of God; he or she has the capacity for the infinite, for things having no frontier.

The common division between believers and nonbelievers does not stand up therefore to the most elementary logic. The logic derives from a bowdlerized translation of the insulting distinction between believers and infidels. In effect, those who believe in A (which they call God) call themselves believers while calling those who do not believe in A unbelievers. This attitude is unilateral and calls those who believe in B unbelievers. This is merely a distinction of power. Why should A be the criterion of division and not B?

Christian philosophy distinguishes between *credere in Deum,* "to believe in God" (opening to the mystery), *credere Deo,* "to believe God" (to have confidence in what a supreme Being has said), and *credere Deum,* "to believe that God is" (to believe in God's existence). As for faith, it has no object. Thought has an object. If faith had an object, it would be an ideology, a fruit of thought. God is not an object, God is not a being, nor even the supreme Being. God is not the chief, one who commands. Divinity surges forth beyond thought. Without a mystic sense, therefore, we deform almost automatically, without intending to, a series of experiences. We deform that experience of a "more" that is found in every human being. I remind readers here that we are speaking about God and not Abrahamic monotheism, which we will deal with in a separate chapter.

The *act of faith* is that activity by which we put our faith into practice. It is the act that surges from the heart as symbol of the whole person and through which we make a leap to the third dimension, in which the human being is realized. The act of faith is a saving act—without going further now into a definition of salvation. The act of faith is not a conditioned reflex; it is a free act that does not cut us off from the human condition but, on the contrary, allows it to attain its plenitude.

*Belief*, moreover, is the formulation, the doctrinal articulation, generally announced by a collectivity, which has crystallized progressively during the course of time in propositions, phrases, affirmations, and, to use the Christian word, dogmas or doctrines. Belief is the more or less coherent symbolic expression of the faith, often formulated in conceptual terms.

Doctrinal articulation and conceptual expression are accompanied by institutionalization. The latter often has acquired a negative connotation as an obstacle to the fundamental experience of faith. Religion is above all a constitutive dimension of being human; in consequence, the experience of God nourishes men and women in spite of the difficulties that institutions may cause. Besides, since humans are social animals, institutions are necessary.

In the face of certain forms of institutionalization and abuses of power, there can be reasons for indignation and protest but not for scandal. We should understand that obstacles are part of the human condition, that we live in a world called by the medievals the *regnum dissimilitudinis* (the kingdom of difference), which does not mean the kingdom of contradiction or necessarily of sin, but the kingdom of disharmony, of difference from the divine. We should interpret institutions not as a refuge that would spare us or permit us experience but as a stimulus to make that experience grow, be nourished and reawakened. This requires a considerable degree of maturity.

We ought to recognize institutionalization as a constantly open process. Only the conservative fossilization of established experiences ends in becoming an obstacle; of itself, institutionalization is a necessary human process. We must see this sociological dimension as the crystallization or manifestation of an experience, that the experience is not exhausted or fixed in its structure, and that this structure makes it possible for others to have access to this experience. The purpose of the institution is to make transparent the experience that establishes it. But experience is incarnated in a human being who never stops changing and developing. For that reason the institution ought to adapt itself in order to remain transparent in a perpetual process of transformation.

Belief, in contrast to faith, can be lost. For example, belief in a particular formulation can be lost: *Actus fidei non terminatur ad enuntiabile, sed ad rem,* says Saint Thomas ("The act of faith does not find its end in what is declared but in its object").

Dogmas are channels, instruments, through which we try to spy out the mystery. If the constellation changes, or if we no longer are capable of capturing the mystery by means of those channels, it will be necessary to change them. The finger of Buddha points to the moon, Buddhist tradition says, allowing us to discover it, but we should not remain petrified while looking at the finger—or at the heavens, like the "men of Galilee" after the Ascension (Acts 1:11). Prophets and angels are both necessary, but we should not adore them.

In brief, the experience of God generally occurs through the mediation of a belief but should not be identified with it.

## The triple horizon of divinity

Divinity repeatedly has burst into the human being, as history shows. That is why, instead of trying to describe these "descents" of the divine, we limit ourselves here to mentioning the various ascents of the human spirit to the mystery of divinity.

Reflection on the horizon of intelligibility in which we evolve seems indispensable for understanding our subject. Each culture provides us with this horizon since it offers us the environment of intelligibility in which things and events take on meaning. That is why we define culture as the inclusive myth that reigns in a given time and space.

Phenomenologically speaking, the function of divinity is to confer an ultimate frame of reference. We are able to situate this center beyond the universe or in its own center, in the depths of the human (our intellect or our heart), or, quite simply, nowhere. Cosmology, anthropology, and ontology offer us the three principal horizons in which the divine appears.

*The cosmological horizon*

Human beings, especially but not exclusively in antiquity, lived face-to-face with the world. The universe, as an animated habitat, constituted their center of interest. Their regard was directed to the objects of heaven and earth. It was in that horizon that divinity appeared, not simply as one thing among others, but as its Lord, its Cause, its Origin or Principle. Its place is at the apex of cosmology.

Divinity appeared linked to the world; it is the divinity of the world, and in turn the world is interpreted as the world of divinity. The functions we suppose are exercised by divinity, and the links that knot us to the world, have in all cases been brought together in the different cosmologies. Divinity is perceived as one pole of the world.

We can say the same thing by making use of an essentially temporal metaphor. Divinity would be at the beginning, prior to the start of everything, just before the Big Bang, the alpha point. Or it would come at the end of the total evolution of the physical universe, the omega point. Or divinity would indeed be the two points at once, alpha and omega, at both the beginning and the end of the universe.

The most widely used name for this divinity is *God*, expressed in some of God's attributes: "Creator of heaven and earth" (Gen. 1); "Varuna supreme Lord, master of the spheres (Rigveda, I, 25, 20); "He from whom all beings are truly born, through whom all live and to whom all return" (Taittirîya *Upanishad* III); as the *Pantokrator* of numerous traditions, both Eastern and Western. Even the *Deus otiosus* belongs to this group. Divinity is a cosmological category. Its dominant trait is power. God is the supreme architect, the all-powerful engineer.

## The anthropological horizon

At a specific moment of history, the principal interest of humanity ceased to be nature and the surrounding world and became centered on the human being itself. Our glance concentrated on interiority: feelings and mind. The location of divinity moves to the kingdom of the human. Its place becomes anthropological.

Divinity, then, is perceived as the real symbol in which the perfection of the human being culminates. This notion of divinity is not so much the fruit of a reflection on the cosmos or an experience of its divine nature as the culminating summit of the consciousness we have of ourselves. Divinity is the plenitude of the human heart, the real destiny of humanity, the guide of all peoples, the beloved of mystics, the lord of history, the complete realization of what we really are. Divinity has no need to be anthropomorphic, although it can present some human traits. In this instance divinity is *âtman-Brahman,* the completely divinized man, the Christ, Purusha, or even the symbol of justice, peace, or the perfect society. Here it can be considered as immanent or transcendent. Whether identified with humanity or separate from it, Divinity's functions are understood in relation to the human being. This is the living divinity, loving or threatening, who inspires, is concerned, punishes, rewards, and pardons. Every journey ends in this divinity, every distance disappears, every sin is annulled, every thought beats a retreat. Divinity is a metaanthropological category.

The dominant trait of this horizon is freedom. Men and women experience liberty, but in a limited and often painful form. Freedom, whether we understand it as salvation or in some other manner, is a human ideal. Divinity is itself liberty and therefore liberates us. Modern theologies of liberation belong in this framework. Divinity is what is at work in history.

## The ontological horizon

The culmination of human development is the consciousness of transcendence. The power of reflection makes *homo sapiens* the superior beings we believe ourselves to be. In this framework the place of divinity is that of a super-being. Its place would be metaontological, beyond Being.

Human beings are proud of their capacity to recognize that they cannot understand everything. Divinity then is perceived as not only beyond the physical world but also beyond the confines of every natural domain, including the human world (intellect, desires, will), or whatever else. It will not even be called *natura naturans* (or "nature naturing," as Averroës and Spinoza conceived it) or *ungenaturte Natur* ("unbegotten nature," in Meister Eckhart), because it is not *natura*. The transcendence or otherness is so absolute that it transcends itself and cannot even be called transcendent. Divinity is not; its being is beyond Being. Its place is metaontological. It is not even Non-Being. Its apophatism is absolute. Silence is our only attitude, not because of the fact that we cannot speak of divinity, but because its specificity consists in being silence. This silence neither hides nor reveals. Divinity is silence because it says nothing; it has nothing to say. A possible name for this divinity is *nirvâna* or "Neither-Being-Nor-Non-Being." Another name is the *mia pêge theotêtos* (a single source of divinity) of the Christian Fathers, adopted at the Fourth Council of Toledo (638), when they came together to call the Father *fons et origio totius divinitatis* (source and origin of all divinity). Divinity is perceived here as a metaontological reality. Every thought on its subject would be idolatry.

Here the dominant trait of divinity is the mutual relation between immanence and transcendence. A transcendence without its corresponding immanence would be contradictory and irrational. We cannot mention even a pure transcendence without destroying it. An immanence without transcendence would signify the inexpressible and unintelligible tautology of an identity that would not even be able to be one for itself. In effect, we cannot even affirm *A* because that affirmation, if we desire it to be intelligible, would be equivalent to *A=A*; that is to say, the copula projects the first *A* toward the second in order to affirm its identity. In other words, the true identity is an immanence that transcends itself. Divinity is precisely that immanence-transcendence that is inscribed in the heart of every being. I am divine in so far as I am what *I am*, and I am not divine in so far as I am *not* what *I am*. All this amounts to saying that an absolutely single Being does not exist. Being is relation. Even the One of Plotinus is not a Substance.

The three horizons—cosmological, anthropological, and ontological—do not exclude each other. Numerous thinkers in many traditions try to approach the mystery of divinity by encompassing all three levels. Thus, for example, *nirguna Brahman* would correspond to the third function, *saguna Brahman* would practice the first function, and *isvara* the second. For its part, Christian scholasticism would combine the conception of God as principle of motion (first function) with the personal God of believers (second function) and the God of mystics (third function). All that we have just noted presents an accumulation of philosophical and theological problems that the various traditions try to resolve in different ways.

By means of these three ways, humanity, throughout its history, has expressed its intention of transcending itself and of recognizing the existence of a mystery that is beyond intelligibility and that, in a certain manner, is present in us. We cannot understand the unintelligibility (that would be a contradiction!), but we can be conscious of it.

## Fragments on the experience of God

Everything that we would be able to say about the experience of God in a strictly rational manner would be blasphemous. Indeed, there is something blasphemous about every theodicy and every form of apologetics. To want to justify God, to prove God's existence or even defend God, implies that we are presenting *ourselves* as the very foundation of God. We are transforming ontology into epistemology, and the latter in a logic that would be above the divine and the human. Ultimately, it is a question of the primacy of thought over being, which has characterized Western thought since Parmenides.

The experience of God cannot be monopolized by any religion or any system of thought. Inasmuch as it is ultimate experience, the experience of God is one that is not only possible but even necessary for all human beings to arrive at the awareness of their own identity. Human beings are fully human only from the moment that they experience their ultimate foundation, what they really are.

The experience of God is not the experience of whatever or whoever there might be. It is not the experience of an object. The whole Christian tradition, from Denys the Areopagite to Thomas Merton, as well as the majority of the religious traditions of humanity, have always told us that we can only know one thing about God: that we cannot know him. "Blessed be the one who has arrived at infinite ignorance," says that great genius of the Christian world, Evagrius of Ponticus. *Agnosia* is learned ignorance, absolute non-knowledge. In the *Kena Upanishad* (II, 3), we are sent back to the same experience. We call it God in order not to break completely with those traditions that have utilized this word as symbol of mystery. But perhaps it would be preferable to dispense with it, as we suggested at the beginning of this book.

The experience of God is not the experience of an object. There is no object *God* of which we can have the experience. It is the experience of nothingness, hence of the ineffable. It is the experience of discovering that one's own experience does not arrive at the depths of any reality. It is the experience of emptiness, of absence; the experience by which one becomes conscious that there exists a "something more," but not in the quantitative order, not something that completes but something that has no bottom—an emptiness, a Non-Being, a "something more," if you will, that precisely makes experience possible.

The experience of God is not a special, still less a specialized, experience. When we wish to have the experience of God, when we wish to have an experience of any kind, we inevitably deform it, and it escapes us. Without the links that unite us with all reality, we are unable to have the experience of God. In the experience of eating, drinking, sleeping, loving, working, being with someone, giving someone good advice, doing something stupid, and so on, we discover the experience of God. Since it is not the experience of an object, the experience of God is pure experience; it is precisely the contingency of being with, living with, since it is not the experience of an "I am" but of a "we are." In Christian language, we call it Trinity.

The experience of God is the root of all experience. It is the experience in depth of all human experiences and of each of them: of the friend, of language, of conversation. It is the experience beneath every human experience: pain, beauty, pleasure, goodness, agony, coldness. . . . It is beneath every experience in so far as it shows us a dimension of the infinite, of the unfinished, of the non-achieved. It is beneath every experience also in that it escapes complete expression in any idea whatever or in any sensation or feeling.

The experience of God, in Christian terms, coincides paradoxically with the experience of contingency. The very root of that word suggests this: *cum tangere,* "to touch the tangent." It is in the recognition of tangentiality, when we touch its very limits, that our consciousness opens and we perceive a "beyond," something that escapes our own limits, that transcends every limitation. This experience is fundamentally so simple that when we want to explain it, we complicate and deform it, and it is then that comparisons arise. But this experience eludes all comparisons.

In this context of contingency and its recognition by us, the prayer of petition (*plegaria*) finds its place. Etymologically, *plegaria* is related to precariousness. Prayer arises from our awareness of such precariousness.

There are two types of prayer: there is the praise of one who adores, a kind of thanks from one who finds herself saved; and, second, there is the cry of human alarm from all those who suffer injustice and pain. The two are necessary and inseparable: through the regeneration that is produced in the person and is manifested in praise, this same person recognizes her precariousness. It was the perplexity of Martin Luther, the intuition of *simul justus et peccator,* "simultaneously a just person and a sinner." In recognizing this radical ambivalence of the human being, Luther had his greatest religious experience and came to recognize that his inner conflict finds its solution in Christ. And he held on to his position; that, he felt, was the human condition.

To recognize this human condition as both precarious and glorious is to recognize that this experience overturns all our values. And it is precisely this rupture of our assumptions that opens us to freedom and prevents us from hanging on to whatever there may be and judging on the basis of it. "Do not judge" (Matt. 7:1; Luke 9:37); there is the beginning of freedom and the joy of living.

The experience of God, which is beneath every experience and makes us human, also gives us a consciousness of our contingency, making us humble and capable of understanding. Through this experience, we come to recognize that we are in the interior of something that includes everything. We become conscious of a double dimension of absence and presence, and we become aware of participating in a more in which, in one way or another, we can have confidence. Some will call this the experience of Being, which is actualized in the disinterested love of beings. On other occasions, I have called it "cosmotheandric confidence," which links the cosmos, God, and humans.

Others prefer to say that it is precisely our contact with contingency that brings us to discover the Other, Nothingness, Emptiness, and the Void. To understand that "all is vanity" (Eccles. 1:2; *vanitas, vacuum,* "emptiness"), we ought already to have come to recognize that all is emptiness. "The infamy of vanity covers the absolute reality with its ego," says a verse of the sufi Mohammed Sherin Tabrizi Maghrebi. And the same fifteenth-century master adds in his *Diwân* that support for the dwelling place of unity (monotheism) is found in the *kenosis* (*fanâ*) of the ego.

Such is the experience of God that, as we already have said, cannot be a specialized experience; it requires all our being and our whole being:

• all our being: intelligence, will, feelings, heart, reason, attachment;

• our whole being: our non-fragmented being.

If we are not unified, if our experience goes in one direction and our body in another, if our feelings push us from one side and our desires from the other, our experience of God will be so fragmented that it will no longer be the simple experience of God.

The indispensable condition for receiving the experience of God is for our whole being to be unified. Chinese wisdom tells us this in a simple metaphor: "When the gong is well forged, whatever be the manner in which you strike it and deal it blows, it will always respond with a harmonious and well-distributed sound." When the person is unified, "well forged," whatever blow it may receive, he or she will always transmit a harmonious vibration, in the same manner as the gong.

We ought to be in harmony with ourselves and with the universe in order to speak properly of that which, precisely, is at the basis of every human experience. Every discourse and every theology from which this experience is absent is nothing but verbiage, the simple repetition of what we have been told, of what we have memorized, of what we do not know for ourselves.

The problem of revelation is manifest here. The difficulty of revelation is not in what God reveals, nor in what is said to us in revelation, but in what I am able to understand of what has been told me in revelation. Thomas Aquinas repeatedly notes, *Quidquid recipitur ad modum recipientis recipitur,* "Whatever is received is received according to the mode of the one who receives it." Revelation is neither in the *revelans* (the one who reveals), nor in the *revelatum* (the revealed, the content of the revelation), but in the *revelanti* (to whom it is revealed). Revelation is in the one who receives it. The problem is in the receiver.

The experience of God is not an experience of "I." One of the most striking characteristics of the twentieth century is the process of "psychologization" that has taken place in the most diverse domains of human life. And religious experience has not escaped the influence of this process. Psychoanalysis has structured the human psyche in three areas in which the unconscious has acquired great importance.

In regard to the experience of God, many began to pose questions on the relation between this experience and the depth experience of the I, composed of something "more" than will or reason. The experience of God is obviously linked to that experience of the deep ego but is not reduced to it. To interpret it with the categories of the deep ego supposes that one has overcome rationalism, in the sense of arriving at a very positive existential experience. But life is not limited to the conscious, and I am not simply an individualized "ego," separate from all the rest. There is also in me an unconscious and a subconscious, and I participate in the archetypes of humanity, which open me to the mystery.

But the experience of God cannot be interpreted even as a pure psychological phenomenon that would not transcend the frontiers of the archetype and the deep ego. It is an ontic and ontological experience: it is an experience of beings and of Being in their most radical identity. It is an experience that surpasses me and my usual modes of experience. Roles are exchanged: I am no longer its subject but discover myself in the experience itself. Ultimately, it is mystical experience, the experience of depth. I do not discover another object or other beings; I discover the dimension of depth, of the infinite, of liberty, that is found in everything and everyone. That is the reason why, almost inevitably, the experience of God confers humility, on one hand, and on the other, freedom.

I arrive at God if I do not stop at myself; that is, if my deep I is transported, so to speak, into a thou (we would even say the thou of God). Otherwise, I can fall into a destructive spiritual narcissism. That is why spiritual life is dangerous, ambivalent, and constantly ambiguous. The experience of God liberates me from all fear, including the fear of the destruction of myself, the negation of myself. "It is not I who lives, but Christ who lives in me" (Gal. 2:20). It is with these words that Saint Paul expresses this existential experience that what is deepest in me is Christ, "not an *alter Christus* but *ipse Christus*, not another Christ but *Christ himself*." Negation should not be feared. The fear of the total negation of oneself is the evident proof that this fearful self is not the genuine and authentic thou. The thou rests confidently in the ego.

On this relation between the experience of God and the experience of the psychological ego, two further observations may be pertinent.

The first corresponds to a phenomenological description of God, intended especially for the new generations, who do not seem very interested in these themes: God is that which breaks our isolation while respecting our solitude. God breaks your isolation, God enters into you, you are no longer isolated. At the same time God respects your solitude and permits you to be you, yourself, and not your identity papers, or your mask as father, brother, sister, friend, coreligionist, or whatever identity. This is the *beata solitudino,* the blessed solitude in which I am truly myself, because God is not the being who closely examines me but the one who permits me to be myself to the fullest. In other words, when I am genuinely alone, I encounter God not as object but as *intimior intimo meo,* to speak as Saint Augustine, "the most intimate aspect of myself," what is most interior to me, what I most truly am, and what then, precisely, opens me to others.

That is the reason why traditional counsels emphasize that without personal withdrawal, without solitude, I am not myself and ultimately will find neither myself, nor others, nor God. We will be able to reach the heart of reality and be ourselves only by removing the masks that often define us as an "I."

The second observation refers to the text in which Yahweh asks Abraham to leave his land, his country, and the house of his father (Gen. 12:1). To depart from his own land, his own home, requires that the person be detached from himself, from his own personality. The experience of God is risky; it overthrows our categories and we don't know where it is leading us or where it will end up. In our search for the experience of God we can be sure only that it will have little to do with what we previously expected.

Other religious traditions, although very removed from contemporary psychology, have also taken as theme of reflection this relation between the experience of God and the experience of the ego. In Vedanta, for example, the experience of God is the experience of the I, at which we arrive when we ask, "Who am I?" *Ko'ham?* In trying to answer that question, I begin to discover that I am a mystery. I am not my body, which changes and fades. I am not my thought, that little psychological "I" that is always being transformed. I search for this me, the ultimate subject of all things, but I can say nothing without my ceasing to be subject and without my being transformed into a predicate. In arriving at the true experience of "I am," *aham Brahman,* I participate in the ultimate and unique experience of the one subject of every operation, which is obviously not my ego.

I would like to conclude these scattered reflections on the experience of God with a phrase that expresses the rupture such an experience provokes in any framework that is purely rational: God is known by those who do not know him, and unknown by those who know him (*Upanishad II, 3*). This could be translated by citing Gregory of Nyssa in almost literal terms: "Those who believe they know God do not know him and those who do not know him know him." Recall also this *koan* (paradoxical phrase) of Christ on the prayer of the publican and the pharisee: "This man [the former] went home again at rights with God; the other did not" (Luke 18:9).

The phrase of the *Kena,* confirmed by the *Baghavad Gita* and numerous other texts from the most diverse traditions, justifies our also making this remark: we who are so wise that we know that we do not know are doubly unhappy, because those who do not know it, know it, and those who know it believe they know it although they do not know it, and are consequently at peace. But as for us "intellectuals" who know that we do not know it, there is no one who can save us. We need to discover a new innocence.

The poets always know how to say it better, as John of the Cross reminds us:

> This knowing-ignorance
> is of such great power
> that scholars are never able
> to vanquish it by arguments;
> because their knowing does not know
> how to understand without understanding,
> *transcending every knowledge.*

## Of initiation

After this sketch of the experience of God, there emerges the most urgent and most typical demand, although hardly the only one, coming from the technocratic mentality: *How* do we arrive at this experience? To affirm that we all have access to it, that everyone possesses it though few realize it, only shifts the question: How does one come to know it? Or rather: Do we really have need of it? Perhaps no, for those who do not "know" it; perhaps yes, for those who are searching for it.

Whatever the case, one thing is certain. We do not arrive at this experience through will, as the *Kena* affirms in a reductive manner and Saint Paul confirms. To desire *nirvâna* disqualifies one from attaining it. Everything belongs to another order, that of grace, as many schools affirm. Everything is linked to the whole, *Sarvam sarvâtmakam,* Shivaism affirms. But we cannot deal with everything, still less not all at one time.

We will limit ourselves here to one remark. It is a matter of attending to a characteristic that is present in the greater part of the traditions of humanity but relatively absent in modernity, for the latter finds itself mired in a metaphysical dualism as well as an anthropological individualism. I am referring to what should be called the *sacramental* or *tantric* vision of the universe, if we could liberate these two words from their superficial interpretations and superstitious degeneration.

I accept as such only the vision of the world that does not divide reality into matter and spirit and does not sacrifice the first on the altar of the second (idealistic spiritualities of all kinds), nor the second on the altar of the first (empiricist materialisms of all kinds). In this tantric or sacramental vision, the word is efficacious in the world of the spirit, thought exercises an influence on matter, the senses are spiritual, the divine is incarnated, and the human is impregnated with divinity.

On this point we will mention again only one example in relation to the question that occupies us.

All traditions propose a preparation for the different states of life, whether they be intellectual, social, or religious. For example, the Vedanta and the church fathers say that without faith, it is not possible to do theology; entry into the Platonic academy requires the knowledge of geometry; entry into the religious life calls for a novitiate; initiation into adult life begins with the use of reason and the awakening of sexuality; acceptance by a guru requires a prior ceremony; the very entry into certain communities requires circumcision; the practice of medicine requires a diploma; and the priestly function cannot be exercised without a prior consecration. All these traditions believe that reality is hierarchical, that there are levels of participation, that reality is interdependent, and that this is so because reality is "solidly" assembled.

Solidarity and hierarchy are thus two presuppositions that give meaning to initiation. The latter consists in passing from one level to another (which may well be from one level of awareness to another) by virtue of an action "initiated" by an adequate agent, generally human. Initiation only has meaning in the framework of a hierarchical and interdependent world. Outside of it, initiation degenerates into superstition. To speak of initiation in a world where there is a supposedly egalitarian and individualistic mentality would be a piece of nonsense as well as an anachronism.

In the framework of an interdependent world, initiation is possible because it merely actualizes the "ontonomy" (not heteronomy or autonomy) of each being. Initiation does not cause harm or alienation; it is a manifestation of the dynamism of being. The action of one being on another is possible because the very structure of reality is interdependent—that is, constitutive; *pratitysamutpâda, karma, corpus christi mysticum, umma*—each of these notions is a fundamental idea for four great religions. Of course, that does not prevent the fact that the abuse of power or other causes can introduce initiations that are contrary to nature and produce antihuman attitudes.

In the framework of a hierarchical world, taking hierarchy in its etymological meaning (of sacred order), initiation is necessary because the leap from one state to another, from one degree to another, from one level to another, is not automatic. A collaboration is necessary between a hand that extends itself and arms that are raised to grasp that hand.

Initiation is established in traditional societies that are conscious of the interdependent and hierarchical character of reality. They consider that the human path to perfection calls for a series of steps for "progress" on the ladder of being. That said, a well-defined initiation is the normal path to the experience of God. And even in extraordinary cases, as in Paul's legendary fall from a horse, or hearing a voice that comes from on high, or suffering a simple personal misfortune, there can be initiatory factors. In any case, the normal path is that of human initiation. It is up to fathers and mothers, teachers, elders. In our time of familial, psychological, and social crisis, we have a need of genuine masters who can initiate their fellow creatures into the experience of God.

It is appropriate here to mention the personal responsibility of those to whom we have just alluded. To those who deplore the eclipse of God, especially among the young generation, we must ask what they have done to initiate their children, students, relatives, or close friends into that ultimate wisdom of life we have called "the experience of God." In spite of all the obstacles presented by a desacralized and individualistic society, and the sarcasm with which a young person may respond to the blessing of the old (perhaps because the latter were not sufficiently transparent to the light they had received), are not we ourselves the opaque body that provokes the eclipse?

We introduced the theme of initiation while raising the question of *how*. There is a reason for that, which goes as much against the dominant culture as what we have said before. Initiation is personal. There are no all-purpose recipes, no prefabricated remedies. All the formulas ought to be authoritative, for the same reason that we call doctors physicians: not because they are experts in industrial pharmacopoeia but because they know how to recommend a personally appropriate medicine. That is a good example of what I mean. But how is one to offer a guide to the experience of God? How, the Eastern masters ask, can one communicate the flavor of tea? Not with a great deal of pondering or austerity, the *Upanishads* reply. "Come and see," says the master of Nazareth. "Tramping along without a path," says the poet Antonio Machado, echoing the teaching of Abhinavagupta, Saint John of the Cross, and many others.

Initiation is personal, we have just said; and the experience of God, as we said at the beginning, is also personal. The way is unique for each pilgrim. Maybe all roads lead to Rome, but there is no sure route that guides you to heaven. Its kingdom is found in mysteries, as we are also told. In a word, there is no one how, no recipe, no broad highway to be followed. This is precisely the job of the master and the function of initiation. The mother says one thing to her adolescent son and another to her daughter who is about to be married; the master takes us by the hand to help us clear personal paths, which are usually quite different; the mantra is secret and personal (and it is not a magical formula, despite the danger it runs of becoming one); the water of baptism bathes the body of each child to be baptized even if it is a matter of a collective ceremony.

If the experience of God is such as we have suggested, it cannot be sold in any market, even if the market is called a temple. Someone got very angry, twenty centuries ago, in a case of that kind.

We say that it is up to each generation to initiate those who come after it in the experience of God, which is the experience of true life. Neither the reading of a book, nor radio, nor television, nor the Internet can be substituted for the personal factor. Perhaps a glance or an embrace can do more than a book, and a living and lived example more than a film, however edifying it may be.

Let me be permitted a brief theological digression. The human being, almost all the traditions say, is the priest of nature, the mediator between heaven and earth. He or she is neither God nor pure animal, neither divine nor earthly, neither angel nor beast, as Pascal said. We do not possess our nature, as things do, because we have to forge it ourselves, wrote Pico de La Mirandola. According to a certain Judeo-Christian exegesis, we are the kings of creation (despite abuses); a "third world between God and nothingness," scholasticism declared; neither just one more thing nor their creator, as the Greeks, the Indians, and the Chinese perceived; and neither divine nor natural, as the Africans teach. As philosophical reflection affirms, we are not finished beings.

We are interdependent beings. In order for us to realize our lives fully, whatever they may be, since succeeding in becoming truly human is not simply a biological development, we have to be prepared for such a life by someone other than ourselves. None of us gives life to ourselves. That is where initiation is situated. No one initiates oneself.

This initiation has numerous degrees and levels. The first degree is the very fertilization of the human being (without for the moment discussing precisely when this takes place); the second is birth. But we only fill the first condition when the child is deliciously passive. There is not yet anything that can properly be called initiation. Initiation begins with the step from *bios* to *zoê,* from pure physical-chemical biology to humanly conscious life (without entering further into details).

We are the priests of the earth, I have said. This priesthood or mediation between the two worlds begins with the first initiation, which has as many names as there are different cultures.

The first initiation transforms the child into a being reborn (as in Hinduism); as a member of the whole chosen people (Judaism); into a complete adult as son of God, as Christ (Christianity); into a member *sui juris* of the community (Animism). It is then that human life, properly speaking, begins. But initiations do not end there. In spite of trivialization in many cases, confirmation, marriage, ordination, and extreme unction are other initiations within Christian tradition. (We give this example because, until recently, studies on initiation have been limited to initiation rituals among so-called "primitives" or in secret societies.) Varro in his *De re rustica* (III, 1, 5) calls *initia* the "mysteries." And we know that the Greek word that is used (*teletête*) means "perfection, plenitude."

Without pursuing these historical-religious paths any further, our proposal is the following: an animal cannot have the experience of God in the sense that we are giving these words. In order for us to realize this experience, we have to achieve the fullness of our humanity (in its various degrees, which are not rigidly graded). The reminder that "It is not good for man to be alone" does not mean only that we all have need for company (to share bread). It also means that there is a horizontal community with other human beings and a vertical community in two directions, on the higher level with the divine and on the lower with the earth itself. Let me say this again in different terms: the experience of God occurs in and with the totality of reality, while directly touching on three worlds, in what many sages have called the "mystical key."

In Vedantic spirituality they speak of *paramparâ*, more specifically of *guruparamparâ*, that is, of tradition and the spiritual line, or the line of initiation that unites concrete persons to a master who has initiated them until their arrival at *âdinathâ*, at God, whether one calls God Shiva or some other name. Jesus refers constantly to this line of initiation when he speaks of his Father whose spokesman he is, thereby guaranteeing his testimony, and from whom he receives his authority. The fundamental function of the church, looked at from this perspective, is to keep alive this transmission, this initiation, which, through Christ, goes back to the ultimate mystery of reality. That is what we mean when we say that the church is *sacramentum mundi*, a sacrament of the world, which is a translation of the original phrase for "cosmic mystery." What has been done as a result are only historical and bureaucratic additions. We need water, fire, and the Holy Spirit, and we invoke them in the initiation of baptism. Because Jesus did not belong to the priestly tribe of Levi, the Catholic priest, in a break with Jewish tradition, is ordained Levi while invoking Melchisadech, not as priest of Yahweh but of "the Most High."

We are human, that is, something more than a species of animal, precisely through that initiation that renders us, in scholastic terms, *capax Dei*. Animals do not have the experience of God.

It would be appropriate, no doubt, to be prudent wherever and whenever initiation still signifies something. The function of the initiated is double. On one hand, they should keep alive a living awareness of their guru, their godfather and godmother, their bishop, their mentor, their professor. At the same time they should continue the tradition in a creative manner. Initiates should not follow their masters blindly, whoever these masters may be, or constantly return to them to find shelter under their authority. Initiation is not magic. It requires the freedom of those initiated—which also confers a responsibility on them. The guru is only a channel, a mediation. No authentic masters keep for themselves the authority that came from "on high." *Nârâyanam patmabhuva . . . ,* begins the Sloka of *Advaita Vedânta.* The line of the masters has its origin in the divine mystery itself.

## Passive attitude: yin

We can, however, say more about the how of initiation, a strict corollary of what we have just presented. When insisting before that there is no *how,* we were not defending some kind of anarchical individualism that asserts that "each minor master has his own little treatise." In the first place, genuine masters have read many books, although they do not follow any of them blindly. Mothers do not learn to be mothers in hygiene classes or courses in child psychology (though these studies are certainly very useful) but by giving birth to their child, feeding it, and living with it. A second, and principal, reason for caution about the how is more basic: initiation comes from the outside, we have said, it is an initiation of transcendence. This leads us to put the emphasis on our *responsibility.* The initiative of life comes from life. We cannot give it to ourselves. The initiative for all initiation comes from the Spirit. The initiative for initiation into "the experience of God" comes from God. The classic mystics refer to *Pati divina*—that is, to suffer the impact of the divine initiative. This leads us to reassert the value of the passive attitude in the face of our problem, without falling into the opposite extreme or accepting degrading abuses.

Our knowledge does not lead us to the goal, nor does our will or our desire open us to the experience of God. God cannot be the answer to any question: we would be making God an idol, an object, a concept. If God is superior to us, the initiative has to come from God. That is probably why Huang Po asserted, "Don't look for the truth. Your very search would destroy what you are looking for." He is telling us that the *yang* (masculine principle) would destroy the *yin* (feminine principle), that God is not the object of research. As all the mystics know, the attitude before God is more passive—should one say feminine? It is truth that searches for us.

An endemic sin of humanity with millennial roots is cultural patriarchy, the often despotic and more often unilateral domination by one part of humanity. It is a matter, at this ultimate level, of our own forgetfulness in the face of the mystery of reality, of the passive attitude that is neither quietist nor "passivity." An example of this lies in the philosophical reductionism that pretends to have identified reality with ontological revelation, and still worse, to have reduced ontology to a "word of being," a purely rational interpretation of reality that we can dominate through this means. As a consequence, we see the split between epistemology and ontology, the reduction of this new science of knowledge to what I have called "the epistemology of the hunter." In this process we set out with reason as a weapon to see if we can attain our object, capturing and fully grasping it. This masculine epistemology, which eliminates the spirit, is certainly incapable of being applied to God. This is an epistemology that would make us believe we can know without loving.

In certain passages of the Gospel of Luke (1:29, 34, 45; 2:19, 51)—I will resist the temptation to comment on them—the evangelist lets us understand that Mary has not understood much of what happened at Bethlehem, Jerusalem, and Nazareth, but that she "treasured all these things and pondered them in her heart" (2:19). Rational comprehension is neither the most sublime nor the ultimate paradigm of intelligibility. To "ponder all these things in her heart" is to do more than split hairs.

To arrive at the experience of God it is necessary therefore to let oneself be fertilized, be surprised. It is necessary to reverse epistemology: "I know because I am known; I love because I am loved," say both John and Paul (1 John 4:11; Gal. 2:20). This attitude of allowing oneself to grasp and to recognize, of permitting the experience to take place in ourselves, is extremely widespread in humanity. Every experience, understood in its most profound sense, is always passive. It is neither projection nor objectivation; to desire it is of no great help and can even become counterproductive. It is capable of taking place or not taking place, occurring with or without meditation, of being a sudden act or a long process or even a misfortune. We cannot reduce everything to our mental categories.

In still other terms, the expression *experience of God* can be interpreted as a subjective, not an objective, genitive. In fact, it is not my experience of God but God's experience in me and through me of which I am conscious.

The meaning of the subjective genitive refers to the very experience of God who is, as much as God confers it on me and I participate in it, what constitutes the deepest kernel of my being. The experience of God is not my experience of him, and I would not be conscious of that. "My experience" would be, to revert to the metaphor of the hunter, to aim at an object, a reality, which is called God, and to try to experience it. But to pretend to make God fall into my experience seems blasphemous to me.

Rather, the experience of God in the sense of a subjective genitive would be a participation of myself in the experience *of* God. It implies my conscious response and my participation in that experience whose ultimate subject is precisely God. I understand my participation in that experience as a communion, a communion between God, who is the subject, and that experience *of* God that is *mine* to the degree that I become conscious of it.

To accept the experience of God in the sense of a subjective genitive implies understanding that the way leading there does not consist in searching but in discovering by chance. We do not have the initiative. A brief story about Huang Po illustrates this well. A being athirst for God, in search of the experience of God, he goes off into the valley to do penance, to meditate, to prepare himself, to purify himself. But he achieves nothing, finds nothing. Then he cries, groans, and beseeches. When he hears a voice from the top of the mountain, he climbs to the summit of the mountain in order to listen. But once there, he neither finds nor hears anything. He goes back into the valley with the feeling that he is being mocked, that he has been deceived. He cries out and groans again, and again he hears the voice. He climbs back to the summit of the mountain and finds nothing but silence. He descends and climbs, climbs and descends. Finally he becomes silent, stops beseeching, and stops searching. He then becomes aware that the voice that he had heard was nothing but his own echo.

# 3

# CHRISTIAN EXPERIENCE OF GOD

The title of this chapter has no definite article because we do not claim to describe *the* Christian experience of God. Many possible experiences of the divine mystery would have the right to call themselves Christian. We also do not add the indefinite article, for it is not a question of *one*—and only *one*—experience among all those that are possible. My reason for violating grammar is twofold and serious.

In the first place, as we already have said, *God* is not the only name women and men have employed to symbolize this ultimate experience. Even "One" suggests but one among several possibilities. We do not want to become tangled in these theological undergrowths.

The second and more serious reason is the following: in spite of the intimate connection, especially in historical terms, between the two, what is central for Christianity is not so much the experience of God as the experience of Christ. But we do not wish to penetrate further into this christological forest.

## Three visions of God and world

To approach a possible Christian experience of God, it is appropriate first to locate the place of *God* in human consciousness. Let us emphasize here that we are not speaking of conceptions of divinity but of the more concrete problem of the relation of God to the world, for it is in the world that the Christian event will make its appearance. What is this world that God has loved so much (John 3:16) and that we are then ordered not to love (John 16:33; 1 John 21:15-16; John 4:4)? Although these texts refer to two different worlds, when all is said and done, it is the world that the Christian ought to confront. The history of humanity bears witness that human consciousness has approached the relation of God to creatures within three principal frameworks:

• *The dualist vision,* in which God is the "absolutely Other." There is an infinite distance between Creator and creature; there is no way of understanding, as in Vedânta or Thomism, the relation of God with creatures as a "relationship of reason": the unique target of human understanding. Such a God does not deal with human beings, because God is immutable, infinite. We experience God as wholly "Other" precisely because we start with the I as subject of the experience.

• *The monist vision,* which in theological terms would be pantheism. Everything is God, and we all experience God insofar as we all experience things. *Deus sive natura,* Spinoza says: God or Nature. There is no other God than this *natura,* in which the relation between Creator and creature is also that "of reason," but in an inverse perspective. In this context, creatureliness does not imply a distinction from the Creator.

• *The non-dualist vision (advaita),* in which divinity is neither individually separate from the rest of reality nor totally identical with it. The *Upanishads,* for example, present a religious attitude that is based neither on dialogue nor monologue, but on the super-rational experience of a "reality" that in a certain sense "inhales" to the interior of itself.

In the simplest terms, a great part of the wisdom the East offers to the West is the non-dualist vision of reality. Yet this vision also suggests a more complete image of the Trinity. God is neither the Same (monism) nor the Other (dualism). God is one pole of reality, a constitutive pole. Although silent and hence ineffable in itself, it nevertheless speaks to us. It is transcendent but immanent in the world, infinite but delimited in things. This pole is nothing in itself. It exists only in its polarity, in its relationship. God is relationship, intimate internal relationship with all.

Once this is said, though we still can argue, we cannot avoid a definitive choice either for or against one of these three millennial options in human history. None of them can be refuted, although we may find them more or less convincing. It is quite obvious that reason cannot have the last word in a matter where, as part of reality, its own position is itself under question. Otherwise, reason would divinize itself. Even so, we cannot make an abstraction of the limited human being who interprets reason. Nevertheless, the three visions do seek, each in itself, an interior coherence. Here we have a reasonable argument in favor of pluralism. Certain ultimate options cannot be settled by either the intellect or logic. "God has abandoned the world to the disputes of men," says a text from the Latin Bible (Eccles. 31:11).

## Conceiving the divine

In itself, the Christian event constitutes a challenge to both monism and dualism. The principal dogmas of Christianity are non-dualist: Christ is neither uniquely God nor uniquely human; at the same time he is not half-God and half-human.

Neither an absolutely "Other" God, any more than a God who is All, fits into the conception of Christ's divinity. Neither monotheism nor dualism is compatible with the orthodox and traditional conception of the *Incarnation*. The *Trinity* is as much a challenge to monism as to dualism. If there is one and only one God, the Trinity is either superfluous or no more than a simple modality. If there are three gods, the Trinity is an aberration. And if God is neither "one" nor "three," what does the Trinity mean? Precisely that: God is neither one nor three. God does not allow himself to be enclosed in any number. *Qui incipit numerare incipit errare* (Who begins to count begins with a mistake), says Saint Augustine. Hence it is inaccurate to say that God is three persons. The concept of person applied to the Trinity, to Father, Son, and Spirit, is not univocal (three absolutely equal persons would be three Gods), nor is it analogical. As Saint Thomas says, speaking of three persons is a concession to current language and nothing can be called "three" in the Trinity. If I utilize the word *person,* applied to three persons, and the three persons are not equal (that would be a tritheism), they would then be analogues. But if they were analogues, there would have to be a *primum analogatum* (a primary reference in the analogy), superior and prior to the three persons, which founds their analogy and permits us to apply it analogically to *A, B,* and *C.* But if there is a *primum analogatum* distinct from the three analogues *A, B,* and *C,* it would be a matter of something superior to the three persons, above divinity, which would permit us to say that the Father is divine, the Son is divine, and the Spirit is divine. The divinity of the persons would be simple participation. But that would be the famous *quaternitas* that the church condemned, or Gilbert de la Porrée's *divinitas.*

This was also Meister Eckhart's misunderstanding. His *Gottheit* was precisely the "Father." Both Gilbert and Eckhart were too entangled with the metaphysics of the One.

But we have known for a long time and under almost all latitudes that One is not a number; it is rather the symbol of intelligibility. That is the challenge of the Trinity and of non-dualism. The concept of person in the Trinity, therefore, is equivocal. The difference between the "persons" is infinite. There is no divine nature apart from the persons. It is not without reason that the Greeks in the early church controversies preferred the concept of *hypostasis.* The One is neither three nor persons. We just as well could say *sun, person,* and *wind.* But I will not explain now my conviction that the unique divine "person" is Christ. We already have suggested that the Trinity is not a simple, accidental modification of monotheism.

Although the One is certainly not a numerical value, it surely implies the negation of all multiplicity; it is the expression of unity, and is in that way the seat of intelligibility. To say that God is not One means that the rationalizing human mind cannot reduce reality *ad unum,* and at the same time cannot make unity an abstraction. If, in the monotheistic perspective, there is one absolutely omniscient being who embraces and understands all of reality, that is not the case for the Trinity. Nevertheless, there are not three Gods: this is non-dualism. God is not one, but neither is God two, nor any multiplicity. It is only through the constant negation of duality, by the refusal to close the process, in the conscious renunciation of trying to understand everything, in the *neti neti* of apophatic mysticism, that we can approach the trinitarian mystery.

One challenge for the theology of the third millennium will be taking far more seriously than before the mystery of the Trinity. Indeed, what has the Trinity meant until now in the spiritual life of the majority of Christians? They scarcely know what it means, and as a result it has little impact on their personal lives. Nevertheless, the trinitarian vision of reality is nothing less than a human invariant that is found, implicitly or explicitly, in practically all the traditions of humanity. A certain elitist and self-sufficient idea of the Christian Trinity has propagated the idea of a Christian monopoly in regard to the Trinity, thereby reducing it to a clever intellectual game.

God, the Human, and the World are not one, nor two, nor three. They are not three things, neither are they one. There is a radical relativity, an irreducible connection between the Source of what is, that which Is, and its very Dynamism; Father, Son, and Spirit; *Sat, Cit,* and *Ananda*; the Divine, the Human, and the Cosmic; Liberty, Consciousness, and Matter; or however we might name this triad that constitutes the real. Reality is trinitarian, not dualist, neither one nor two. Only by denying duality (*advaita*), without reducing everything to unity, are we able consciously to approach it.

The discovery of the Christian trinitarian God, which is not conceived identically to the God of Jewish monotheism, even if Jews are able to bring precise nuances to this terminology, is the great theological challenge for Christianity in the third millennium.

Certainly the reasons for condemning Jesus were not insignificant. It was not a question of petty quarrels or envies. In my reading, the Jews did everything possible to save Jesus, but he himself renounced the fundamental basis of the Torah. It was a problem of conscience for Israel and not a plot of scoundrels. Jesus was not condemned for calling himself divine, for the idea of human divinization was neither new nor scandalous. He was condemned for proclaiming himself the Son of God in the trinitarian sense of the expression, as it will be interpreted later: the only Son of God—equal to God, proceeding from God. In other words, he was condemned for having defied the people of Israel by presenting himself as the divine icon without having denied his human condition. In the eyes of the Jews, the crime of Jesus was to have dared to supplant Yahweh, the icon of Israel, by putting himself in Yahweh's place, and it was in this way that the Christians of the first generations understood it. If "the people of God" had refused to adore other gods, how much more strongly should they get rid of someone who dared to affirm that the Messiah was not a king in the manner of David but the veritable icon of Divinity, the perfect image of Yahweh, generated directly by God. The rupture with Israel was consummated by what has come to be called the (first) Council of Jerusalem (Acts 15:1ff.), in the course of which the apostles had the audacity to abolish circumcision, the fundamental sign of Judaism (Gen. 17).

But the trinitarian scandal that, according to the theology of the first centuries, cost Jesus his life ended in time by becoming blurred. Some Christian consciences, in an almost imperceptible manner, slipped again, little by little, toward the legalism that Paul denounced with such vigor. This is an important and neglected theme of political theology. The Trinity did not fit in with the Christian empire. Theocracy is more in accord with monotheism. From the doctrinal point of view, the mystico-speculative progress in the approach of the trinitarian mystery was not supported sufficiently by practice and had relatively little influence on Christian life.

The monotheism of orthodox Judaism emerged again in the way Christianity was lived. The God of the Hebrew Bible was identified with the Christian God, and the people of Israel corresponded to "the people of God." For many, Jesus became simply the God of Christians; that is the impression, for example, that Hindus have if they happen to hear the preaching of the gospel. For them, Christians are a people who adore God under the name and form of Jesus.

Our presentation of the Christian vision does not, of course, invalidate other visions; still less does it condemn other religions. Although we are prepared to defend our opinion in the public arena, that would be to reduce the mystery of what we have agreed to call God, if it were indeed possible for us to have the slightest notion of God.

## Distinguishing Christ and Jesus

Christ is the Christian parameter for speaking about God. God has pronounced one and only one word: Christ. This parameter, given to us two thousand years ago, permits us to speak about God—on condition, of course, that we always remain conscious of the cultural and historical burden this parameter entails.

For two thousand years, Christian language has been the biblical language received and interpreted in a Hellenistic context. By *language* I mean not only a tongue and a grammatical structure but also the horizon of intelligibility that language communicates. This language must be understood, transmitted, and eventually translated. Hence there is a triple mediation that prevents us from absolutizing any human affirmation.

To give an example of what Christian theology calls the *preambula fidei*, we say *God* as we might say *history*. It is understood that other cultures and religions have other languages, other perceptions of reality. We cannot interrogate those cultures without first understanding them, and we cannot understand them if our own presuppositions, our particular perspectives, exclude the presuppositions on which those other cultures are based. Intercultural dialogue requires a special methodology that in practice must still be elaborated.

The Christian tradition certainly comes from Jesus. Had there not been Jesus, we would not be speaking of these questions today in such terms. But let us not confuse Jesus with the Christ. Jesus is Christ, and he who confesses that Jesus is Christ obviously is a Christian. It is in and through Christ that Christians find themselves in harmony with all things, with all beings, and with all other men and women. It is Christ the only Son, the Firstborn, Head, Alpha and Omega, Logos from the beginning, through whom everything has been made and who bears everything, as the Christian Scriptures declare. But this Christ is not identical with Jesus. We are so carried away by scientifico-logical reasoning that we think if *A* is *B,* then *B* is *A.*

In an analogical way, if Jesus is Christ, then Christ is Jesus. But this is not so, for Jesus is not *A* and Christ is not *B.* Perhaps the best brief formula would be, "Christ is the risen Jesus." In the eucharist there is the presence of the real Christ, but in the eucharist there are not the proteins of Jesus, son of Mary. Communion is not cannibalism. Jesus is historical and we cannot evade history; yet Christ exceeds the historical, and we cannot diminish reality by reducing it to history.

# Identification and identity

To approach the theme of the experience of Jesus, we must distinguish between identification and identity. Many Christians are satisfied with the identification of Jesus as a man, the son of Mary, who lived in Nazareth and died on a cross under Pontius Pilate, who rose again, and whose existence contains all the other data that tradition has handed down to identify him. We thus know of *what* we speak, but we do not necessarily know to *whom* it is that we refer. The identification of Jesus of Nazareth, which permits us not to confuse him with anyone else, is not the same as his identity, the identity that would allow us to know him.

To know a person's identity, one needs love, one needs faith, one needs to make a personal discovery that would prepare an opening to that identity. In this face-to-face, person-to-person meeting, of thou to thou, of lover to lover, the other is known in his or her unicity and singularity. The one who is known thereby transforms the one who knows, and the one who knows transforms the one who is known. This is the mystery of identity and the person. The mother knows the identity of her son in a deeper way than in the identification the police made at the time he committed a minor theft.

To know the identity of Jesus of Nazareth, we must meet his person. History can only describe important figures for us. We cannot truly encounter the person in the past. We can have a memory of the past, an *anamnesis,* a belief—inevitably a fragile belief—inasmuch as its historical paradigms are but feebly established. We can believe in the events of Bethlehem and in other facts of Jesus' life, although we cannot pretend to have had the experience of Bethlehem, of the incarnation, or of the empty tomb: we were not there and we have not seen them. Experience is not a memory; experience is what happens to us and transforms us. Such an experience can certainly be founded on a memory that has been actualized, in which case it is a matter of a memory that was retransmitted by previous generations.

If Christ is no more than an historic personage, the experience of the Christian is reduced to living the memory of his life, retransmitted by the memory that people have preserved of it. In that case, it is the experts who would have the greatest authority, and Christianity is thereby reduced to being a religion of the Book.

But for the Christian the experience of Jesus is the experience of the risen Jesus—that is, living, *hic et nunc* (here and now), yesterday, today, and always, to use the words of Saint Paul. It is an experience that is transhistorical, not historical; personal and nontransferable. It takes place in time without being simply historical. That is why this experience is so strong yet so difficult to communicate. The act of faith actualizes this experience of the ineffable, which for Christians is realized "in Christ and though him." But those who have not had the experience of being resurrected through Christ, even if they call themselves Christians and are perfectly orthodox (confusing *doxa* and doctrine), still would not be able to say, like the Samaritans to the woman at the well: "Now we no longer believe because of what you told us; we have heard him ourselves and we know that he really is the savior of the world" (John 4:42). Such orthodox Christians would be incapable of understanding the "carnal" aspect of the incarnation, neither the opening of the first chapter of John nor the majority of the texts of Scripture, nor even of Christian tradition. Christianity is not a religion of the Book: it is a religion of the Word, of the living word that is heard and perceived in its transforming force by those who have "ears to hear."

The book of the Acts of the Apostles and the epistles of Paul give us an account of the profound crisis of universalism that the church experienced in the second decade of its history. Are we really able to assert that, twenty centuries later, the church has completely overcome that first crisis of catholicity? The first concept of catholic (*kat'holon* in Greek) would suggest a total religiosity that would include all of life, including what pertains to the body. It offered to all who followed it everything people need for their fullness and salvation (*secundum totum*, in Saint Augustine's translation). It is instructive to note that the word *catholic* came to be interpreted more and more as a geographical and cultural category, much in accord with Europe's expansionist and colonizing spirit. The sociology of knowledge could enlighten us on this point. Is the Christ event essentially linked to the cultural framework of the Mediterranean? Here we are posing the question of Christian identity.

Inasmuch as the word *religion* has several meanings, it is an extremely problematic term. Here we are content to point out that religion (that which links people to themselves, each other, the world, and the divine) includes:

• *religiosity*, the human dimension that permits us to open ourselves to transcendence and faith.

• *religionism*, or the sociology of religion, which refers to or signifies membership in a particular social (church) group, itself held together by a more or less open system of beliefs: Buddhism, Judaism, Marxism, and so on.

• *religiology,* the science of religion, the human reflection on the fundamental beliefs of life, including theology, philosophy, and science.

On one hand, we have a religion called Christianity that is distinguished from all others. On the other, we have an ensemble of experiences (love of God and neighbor, truthfulness, fidelity, humility, openness, freedom) that for Christians are expressed in Christian symbols, and in other cultures and religions in other symbols. I call this Christian religiosity "Christianism," which is not so much a "religion" in a sociological sense as it is the Christian form of humanity's experience of its religious dimension.

After Constantine, Christian consciousness gradually developed into "Christendom," a totalizing conception of religion that includes the political, the social, and the cultural, that is, the culture as a whole (cathedrals, law, the crusades, the Inquisition, the empire, etc.). At the time of the Renaissance, the self-comprehension of Christian peoples liberated itself from political and social monolithism (as a Christian, one does not have to be on the side of the Guelfs or the Ghibellines, the right or the left) and became concentrated on faith, understood preferably as doctrine. This "Christianity" prevails even today. In our time the experimental dimension (or if one prefers, mystical) of the Christian fact, which we have called "Christianness," has appeared with greater and greater strength. It is no longer the juridical (Christendom) nor the doctrinal aspect (Christianity) that is primary, but the lived, personal relationship with the mystery of Christ. It is, of course, a matter of three "kairological" moments of Christian consciousness, and these moments cannot be separated in a simple chronological way.

If, as the exegetes tell us today, for a thousand years Israel experienced a tribal theology, before the prophets made a universal God out of the tribal god of Yahweh, Christians too for two thousand years have experienced a tribal Christology. Now the great challenge is to overcome this tribal Christology by means of a Christophany that would permit Christians to recognize the work of Christ everywhere, without pretending to monopolize the mystery.

None of this means that everyone should be considered a Christian, nor that it is a matter of falling into a panchristic monism. Instead, it permits human consciousness of the last things not to be divided into incommunicable compartments, since a mystical communication exists that cuts across many frontiers. At a doctrinal and even intellectual level, religious systems may be incompatible, religions incommensurable. But people do not live by bread alone, nor on *logos* alone; they live also in the Spirit, which breathes into humanity and the universe where, when, and how it wills. Although Christianity is not the universal religion, Christians are capable of participating, in their own manner, in the ultimate adventure of the universe in and through the particular experience of what they call Christ, and, we should stress, this does not exclude other forms.

In its own manner, each religion can profess a similar project, using other symbols and other denominations. This kind of "ecumenical ecumenism" does not mean that each religion should resign itself to eat only one part of the great dessert at the wedding of heaven and earth, and that everyone should feel satisfied in his or her egoism. Ecumenism does not surrender the *totum,* the plenitude that each religion concretely promises, but is aware that one savors the *totum in parte,* the whole in one's particular part. That is what I have called the effect of the *pars pro toto,* or part for the sake of the whole. Both in my manner of adoring the most primordial totem and in the way I totally consecrate myself to the search for Truth, I am able to enter in communion with the whole of reality in its vital explosion and bring together the most varied metaphors.

## Three texts

Before commenting on three chosen texts (Acts 17:28; John 1:18; and 1 Cor. 15:18), let me mention a fundamental aspect I spoke of earlier. Christian experience arises fundamentally from the interweaving of two traditions, the Semitic and the Greek. If someone is not a Semite spiritually, the specific resonance of the Name of God in whose bosom Christianity emerged is missing. If one is not intellectually Greek, he or she does not have the conceptual framework of person, nature, category, and sin that gave form to the Christian experience of God (at the councils of Chalcedon and Nicea). All these concepts have been created in a concrete geographical and historical context, and they therefore cannot be extrapolated or universalized outside the cultural field in which they have appeared. Christianity's natural ties are to cultures somewhat foreign to non-Western Christians. This creates the already-mentioned necessity of not absolutizing any concrete experience and of reincarnating, in the cultural and vital framework of other contexts, what is radical in the experience of God, and on the other hand of translating the intuitions of other traditions into the terms of the "experience of God."

A great deal has been said for a long time about the "dehellenization" of Christianity, with its ensuing problems, but two thousand years of tradition cannot simply be thrown overboard. But little has been said of an even more serious problem: the "dehebraization" of the message of Christ. We also cannot throw three thousand years of tradition overboard.

To sum it up in one sentence—which must be nuanced with adjectives and adverbs—the Jewish conception of history has limited the Christian God to being the Lord of History while the ontological notion of Hellenism has reduced God to being the Lord of Being. This is precisely the challenge faced by Christians of Asia in this postcolonial period. Can the Father of Jesus Christ be detached from the God of History and the God of Being? Before we rush to respond, let us be careful to avoid the similar temptation of imprisoning the God of Jesus Christ in Asian models. Here is where the question of pluralism emerges in all its sharpness.

A Christian interpretation of the Christian God—putting aside for now an exegesis on the identity the One Jesus of Nazareth called Father—can be expressed through three texts.

*In ipso enim vivimus, et movemur, et sumus,*

"It is in him that we have life, and move, and exist" (Acts 17:28). The three verbs (*we live, we move, we are*) in this sentence refer to the three fundamental aspects of the Christian experience of God.

*We live,* the first verb, sends us back to the fundamental experience of God as life. To say that we live in God can be interpreted as a spatial metaphor, in which God is understood as a kind of atmosphere that envelopes us. This metaphor, however, can lead us to drift toward a distinction that does not correspond to the true experience of God. One metaphor that takes account of this phrase is that of water. We do not wish to say that we live in God as a fish lives in water (even though we appreciate the obvious richness of that expression), but as a drop in the water. To live in God, to have the experience of God, is to recognize ourselves as in him: we live in him, with him, and through him. The drop is visible only outside water, but it is made up of water and the superficial tension that limits it.

*We move*—this second verb speaks to us of the experience of God as movement, energy, and vital principle. It is life as constant dynamism, it is God understood as a force that is not based in ourselves. "We are moved" by God, and not only by God's attraction, as with Aristotle's first unmoved mover. Here, God drags us with him. God is like an empty space that permits us to move.

Finally, *we are* expresses both our being and the fact that we are. It is not enough to say that we have being insofar as we have received it from God. To say that "we are in God" affirms more than that our being has been received from God. If "we are in God," we are so in the degree in which God is and, some would explain, in the degree to which we participate in God.

This life, this movement, and this being of myself in God constitute the true experience of God. The three verbs tell us the same thing by starting from three complementary perspectives. Those who have not lived this omnipresence, this inseparability, and ultimately this divinity in their own being can well have a thought about God, a very sublime thought in fact, but they are not having the *experience* of God. Each of us is a participation, an image, a mystery of God.

*Deum nemo vidit umquam*

"No one has ever seen God" (John 1:18). This second affirmation corrects and completes the first. No one has seen God; no one has dominated God. Vision constitutes one of the basic metaphors of human thought, especially in Mediterranean culture. When Martin Heidegger speaks of the metaphysics of subjectivity, which arose in Greece, he considers vision as the dominant metaphor of this way of understanding reality. Vision supposes objectivization, separation, control, and mastery over that which is the object of the one who sees. Vision expresses that desire of possession that people want to exercise over what surrounds them: God is often represented as an eye that sees everything. In revenge, no one has ever seen God or is able to see God; no one can either control God or know God. God is incapable of being either known or controlled, or what we might describe as reduced to an object, to an experience *of.* We are not capable of knowing God, we are not capable of seeing him; we are capable of savoring God but not of controlling him. Apophatism is not just a luxury for mystics. Everything that falls under the control of our mind is not God. As Meister Eckhart said, the eye with which we see God is the same eye with which he sees us.

*Ut sit Deus omnia in omnibus*

"So that God may be all in all" (1 Cor. 15:28). This text expresses a final end and hence a process. The context of the phrase speaks to us of the mystery of history as the temporal process of *kenosis,* of self-emptying (Phil. 2:7), of divinization. This gives rise to Paul's interpretation in Rom. 8:22, in which all reality is seen as the groaning of a new creation coming to birth, through the ontic and ontological mediation of the Son of God, who subjugates all things to himself before submitting himself to the Father.

In this process of divinization we must take into account two elements that appear in the expressions *all* and *in all*. (They are sometimes evaded in translations that vulgarize the text by trying to be more accessible.) If God is everything, then things themselves disappear. If God is all things, then these things acquire their full value, overcome their individualist isolation, and succeed in being what they are, perhaps because they are no more than on the way (of Being). In that case, however, God simply disappears into an amorphous pantheism. However, if God is all in all things, we again end up with the non-dualist vision.

The universe moves within what the medievals called the dynamism of *egressus* and *regressus* (in a movement of return after its departure from God's bosom), but with a significant difference: divinization is not a simple return to the being of an ecstatic Father, since the Father is only and always Father, that is, begetter. The *regressus* (return) represents an absolute novelty: it is not a last end, it is Being, that in which the whole of reality, indeed *everything*, is involved. Here we enter fully into the mystery of time and historicity. Divinization is not only a final result, understood as departure from and return to the Father. It is also a progressive process of the divinization of each and every component of reality. Time—history— both unites and distinguishes us from the divinity we are. The experience of God is precisely the experience of that tension, of that dynamism made up by the *egress* and *regress* that informs the whole of reality: it is the trinitarian dance or mutuality that the tradition terms *perichoresis.*

# Jesus of Nazareth

The texts of Christian Scripture we have cited allow us to glimpse the perception of God had by those privileged witnesses of the life of the Master. But that does not prevent us from taking a further step toward penetrating the very experience of Jesus, starting with his personal affirmations. We are not examining whether the Gospels accurately convey his *ipsissima verba* (his very own words), or whether they reflect only part of his experience of God. Our procedure is not aimed at clarifying whether he said them or not as in finding a resonance in ourselves for deepening our own experience. At the same time we hope to find some confirmation that he really did say these words; we too are capable of stammering them, even while aware that we dare not pronounce them—even in a low and trembling voice—precisely because he has said them. Here we see again the living circle of *egressus-regressus* to which we have already referred. We are choosing texts in which Jesus speaks in the first person and in which we also find an echo of what the tradition regards as his trinitarian experience.

## *"The Father and I are one" (John 10:30)*

This phrase can be understood literally as the non-dualist confession between the Father and the Son. There is a distinction (the Father and I), while at the same time an internal communion is shown in the fact that they are ultimately inseparable ("we are one"). If we understand Father *as fons et origo totius divinitatis* (the source and origin of all divinity), then this unity between Father and Son shows truly that "water flows." That is to say, life is life because it flows; the Father is Father not only because he names him and recognizes him as Son, but also, and principally, because he generates him, since he does not cease to engender him. If the Father ceased to engender, he would cease to be Father, and the Son would disappear. The Father is only the Father and nothing more. In himself (if this expression is valid) he *is* not; he "*is*" nothing. His very being is an I that constantly engenders and speaks to a thou without, so to speak, any other function or activity. This is the way the tradition of the first Christian centuries understands it. Biological anthropomorphism is capable of bringing us to think of the limited character of divine paternity and of the radical separation between Father and Son. Relations within the bosom of the Trinity are dynamic relations, in constant movement. The Father never ceases to engender, nor the Son to be engendered, and the Spirit is the permanent expression of this dynamism. We participate in this dynamism of begetting inasmuch as we too are begotten. We cannot be simple spectators: Jesus has had the experience of this radical union with the source that gives him that life, to which he gives the familiar name of "papa" (*abba* in Aramaic).

Here we see established the meaning of eucharistic union. It is obvious that although there is but one Son, Jesus Christ, every Christian is called to have the experience, in and through the eucharist, of being fully himself or herself to the degree that he or she participates in the mystery of the Son. The texts are clear (John 6:35 and others). If we cannot have that experience, our Christian commitment is nothing but a more or less interesting indoctrination; we thereby lose the vital root that ought to sustain us as Christians.

This experience of God through the mediation of Christ is crucial: Christ mediator is not an intermediary.

A certain dominant Christian political tradition always has feared divinization precisely because, if one begins with a strict monotheistic presupposition, the latter becomes an aberration. Perhaps this is why many Christians fear achieving the non-dualist experience of unity—that is, the trinitarian experience, with the Father as source and origin of their being. Other traditions are less timorous, perhaps insufficiently. *Aham Brahman* (I am Brahman) could be a seemingly equivalent experience.

"Who has seen me has seen the Father" (John 14:9). This phrase is preceded by, "How long have you been with me, Philip, and still do not know me?" Two thousand years later, we still look for God where God is not present. Jesus tells us that the one who has seen him does not need to see Yahweh because that person has seen the Father. And this vision of the Father in Jesus signifies, and should signify in us too, that the true essence of Jesus is *transparency*. Light is light, and it illuminates well enough to show us its origin. If we place an opaque body in front of it, we no longer see the light.

"Who has seen me has seen the Father." Going back to the commentary above, it is not a question of a Father completely separate from the Son; the Father is father to the degree that he "fathers" inasmuch as he engenders. Thus we cannot see the Father as he might be in himself; we see only the one he has engendered. To say this in a paradoxical way: the Father completely immolates himself, gives himself and disappears in that act, in the Son. What the Father *is,* insofar as he shows himself, insofar as he acts in terms of his essence, is precisely the Son.

What significance does this transparency and this Father-Son relationship have for us? First of all, total transparency is another way of expressing the fact of dying to oneself, of not becoming encysted in the opacity of a life for oneself, prisoners of our own fears, pains, or even joys. It means becoming liberated from egoistic individualism, from an undue appropriation of the life that flows in me. Nothing but transparency is demanded. The experience of God alone makes us transparent.

On the basis of this transparency, we are able to interpret the experience of the living God, which is the experience of the invisible, the experience of nothingness. What is it that lets God become transparent? In the first place, reality as a whole. To the degree we participate in that reality, we will discover God as *fons et origo* (source and origin) and the Son as his plenitude. In the second place, we discover the other, the totally other: the companion, the loved being, the superior, the inferior, the son, the neighbor, the unknown. Who has seen the other has seen the Father. This last affirmation has an immediate application in Christian life. We should not do things for Christ alone, for a Christ separated from other men and women is nothing. Christ becomes transparent in others: therefore our experience of him is not separate from our Christic experience of others—an experience of openness, abandonment, gift, and meeting. "You have done it to me" (Matt. 25:40)—even when we didn't know it.

Paraphrasing the well-known passages of the Gospels, we would be able to say: Who has seen Christ has seen God; the one who does not love his neighbor does not love Christ; one who does not love Christ does not love God. And we speak of loving because, insofar as a person does not love, he or she does not see. "Whoever sees the Dharma sees me" (Itivuttaka, 92) would be the equivalent in Buddhist tradition.

*"It is better for you that I go away, because if I do not go away, the Spirit will not come" (John 16:7)*

The first part of this sentence is in agreement with Jesus' entire life. He flees when they try to make him king; he is not receptive when they call him good; despite his unity with the Father, the latter is greater than he; his life is ephemeral; the experience of God has nothing to do with immutability nor even with the stability of the Absolute. "It is fitting that I depart." There is no question of "putting up three tents" nor of "remaining to gaze on heaven." "Tell no one what you have seen and heard." The ineffable is ineffable. It is only afterward, perhaps, that we can talk about it. The experience of God does not allow itself to be objectified: it is a movement, a passage, a *pascha,* an Easter. Being is a verb and not a substantive; there should therefore be an analogous philosophical formulation. The experience of Being does not consist in imprisoning, seizing, or apprehending it, but in Being being with Being. The experience of God is not a possession but a journey with God being God (*exterior,* "I experience").

The wish expressed by the words "They pressed him to stay with them" (Luke 24:29) is always present in the life of the Christian. But it is precisely in those moments that Jesus disappears. The eucharist, for example, is not the sanctuary but the sacramental act in which Christ appears and disappears in us. There is a Buddhist saying that coincides perfectly with this context: "If you see the Buddha, kill him." If you encounter Christ, eat him. The significance of these two sayings is evident: even that which has been the means of our making progress—if we are too intent on holding on to it, possessing it, and reifying it—can be transformed into an obstacle and a brake. It can become an instrument of mediocrity that prevents us from advancing in our experience, both as Christians and as human beings. As an old Buddhist parable reminds us, it is necessary to abandon the raft made of rushes when we reach the other shore (of _samsâra_). Life is a constant dynamism, just as is the experience of the divine, the continuous divinization of the experience of the real. It is appropriate, therefore, that we remain without a criterion, without a fixed point, without any kind of security. In starting out simply from the experience of "remaining without," of remaining stripped, are we able to be sensitive to the transparency of the divine in everyone and in all of the reality that surrounds us? _Tao k'o tao, fei ch'ang tao_ (the _tao_ that we would be able to call _tao_ is not the authentic _tao_) could be considered an equivalent.

The second part of the phrase speaks of the Spirit. References to the Spirit in the New Testament are numerous: "spirit of truth" (John 15:26); "he who will teach you the way of truth" (Luke 12:12); "it is not you who will be speaking, but the Holy Spirit" (Mark 13:11); "the Spirit of God...living among you" (1 Cor. 3:16). There is no genuine Christian life without the Spirit. But the Spirit does not allow itself to be imprisoned by anything: it is freedom (2 Cor. 3:7).

Christian theology has been suffering for fifteen centuries from what the first Christians called subordinationism, a heresy that constituted the most serious challenge to the Greek mind. It refers to the subordination of the Spirit to the Son, of the third to the second person within the Trinity. Divinity is understood as _logos_; that is how Father and Son are characterized in the prologue to Saint John's Gospel. As a consequence, everything is subordinated to the _logos_ or, what is worse, to rationality. But good sense is unable to accept the subordination of the Spirit, *pneuma,* to *logos.* And when, in our time, one speaks of the theology of the Spirit or pneumatology, the remedy is worse than the sickness. Everything is reduced to the *logos*; even the Spirit has been subordinated to it, except in the tradition of the Russian and some other Eastern churches.

I am not saying that the Spirit can be separated from the spirit of Christ but that the Spirit is not subordinate to the *logos.* We are not able to rationalize or rationally justify the spiritual field. The Spirit is not constrained by rationality, for the Spirit manifests itself as freedom, and we cannot rationalize freedom. The Spirit is unpredictable; we need to be carried away by it. The relation to the Spirit cannot be causal; it should be living, vital.

"It is good for you that I go, otherwise the Spirit will not come." The first part of the sentence can be understood as an abandonment, the desolation that is necessary in order to attain and deepen the experience of God. The Spirit will come in the midst of you, and it will do what it wills; it is the Spirit who will arrange things. The Spirit integrates us into the trinitarian life in a corporeal, personal, contingent manner, in our very person. That is what the experience of God is, our experience within the plenitude of Being. It is then that we are incorporated into the *perichôrêsis* or trinitarian *circumincessio* of all reality. We understand then what Saint Paul is saying when, in letting himself be carried away by the Spirit, he declares Jesus Son of God. And this should help us realize that when we let ourselves be carried away by the Spirit, we arrive at the experience of God itself.

# 4

# PRIVILEGED PLACES OF
# THE EXPERIENCE OF GOD

We can encounter God anywhere. We have only to seek God and hold ourselves ready for the encounter. This is a widely shared thesis. According to classical theology, God is immense, omnipresent. Another equally traditional thesis affirms that God is simple, although it is often forgotten that these attributes should be conjugated simultaneously. God is everywhere, is immense, yet does not have parts: God is simple. This means we can meet God completely in any place whatever. Too often the concerns of life, especially modern life, prevent us from being conscious of this. The fish has a certain awareness of things but does not perceive that he is surrounded by water. Just so, we do not perceive God; we do not go beyond our purely animal consciousness. The animal does not believe in God—he does not believe that he exists in water.

This metaphor permits us to go a little further. The fish does not get wet. It is only when he leaves the water that we become aware (because he dies) that he is drenched. It is knowledge, always the knowledge of good and evil, that shows us we are drenched (by God). And like the fish that dies, only by denying ourselves, by abandoning the idolatry of self, do we discover ourselves drenched, surrounded by

God, as described in a very beautiful way at the beginning of the Isopanishad, among other texts: "The Lord envelopes the totality of the world."

Nevertheless, in some places the water surrounding us is made more manifest than others. We speak of "places" due to the poverty of our language and its incapacity to overcome spatio-temporal paradigms and categories. The metaphor of water helps us. Water (God), for the fish, exists in all places, although perhaps it is detected better in some places than others because, in those places, we perceive more clearly the water that drenches us. But the water that touches us is not seen; what we do see is the thing that is soaked. The experience of God is not the experience of an object, not even of a special "object." It is the experience of the divinity of the thing, but not in the form of an accident "glued" to it. Here, however, the metaphor of water is no longer helpful to us (it "waters"). "God is that in comparison (with which) substance is an accident and the accident is nothing," says aphorism VI of *The Book of Hermetic Tradition of the XXIV Philosophers,* a text widely cited and appreciated by Christian scholasticism. We have the experience of God in the thing, as in the Trinity, in whose bosom "persons" are both equal and distinct at the same time, inseparable from it while also identical to the deepest reality of the thing.

After all we have said, it ought to be clear that these meetings with the divine are not always with a personal God as that is commonly understood—without entering here into considerations on the misunderstanding that exists between East and West concerning the personality or non-personality of God. The first generations of Christians criticized "the pagans" because they personified the forces of nature by divinizing them. Recent post-Christian generations reproach Christians for having an anthropological vision of God. In our time, we are perhaps in a position to see the misunderstandings of both. God is not reducible either to a "super-*kosmos*" or to a "super-*anthrôpos*." Here is the root of the *cosmotheandric* intuition.

But then, it will be asked, what precisely do we encounter? A too-rapid response, though not false, is that we encounter Nothingness—that we encounter nothing. Have we not said that God is not a thing?

Another response, that would be necessary to examine at length, would say that we meet the *alter* and not the *aliud* of ourselves: the Other of ourselves without which we would not exist. Let us not confuse the *alter* (symbol of that part of ourselves that is unknown to us) with the *aliud* (that part of ourselves that is distinct from us, which alienates us from ourselves). God is an *alter,* not an *aliud.*

A third reaction would consist in explaining that we meet the âtman, the deepest aspect of ourselves.

Ultimately, the three answers end up saying the same thing: God is nothing other than this *alter* of myself, that is, the Self in its totality.

Perhaps we could say this in another way that would be more consistent with the mind of the West. The place "where" we experience God, by antonomasia, is ourselves, the human being himself or herself—as we have said, the Self. The "drama" of reality takes place between God and the Evil One in an arena that is the human being, as has been described in the very varied colors of world literature. The human person is the meeting (and collision) point in which the dynamism of reality is played out. The privileged "place" is certainly not the animal that we call rational, but the Man that includes Adam or Eve, Job, Gilgamesh, the man that Dante did not dare to name, or Faust—these are only a few representatives, among others. We are talking about the one who is perhaps too hidden in each one of us, and whom only poets, mystics, and a few philosophers are capable of describing for us.

History is the stage on which the battle between the gods and Asuras, God and Lucifer, is played out. The life of Jesus Christ offers us a paradigm in his constant struggle with the demons: this is the drama of redemption. The human vocation is sometimes too great for us. That is why we have belittled God. It is not by chance that Friedrich Nietzsche, who was passionate about Christ, was so obsessed with Greek tragedy.

But our meditation does not seek simply to describe an experience, nor do we wish to linger over these fascinating questions.

As we have already said, to communicate an experience is no minor affair. Let us remember that, according to several schools of Eastern spirituality, the master emerges only when the disciple is prepared. The reading of a book that hopes to communicate something more than information requires the reader to receive the seed in a soil carefully prepared by manure. If the readers are not prepared, the writing will not penetrate their hearts. There exists a brief aphorism in the Yoga-sutra: "It is in the heart that one discovers the knowledge that liberates" (*Hrdaye cittasamvit*, III, 34). This insight is echoed in the *Gîtâ* (VIII, 12) and is elaborated in the Sufist conception of heart (*qalb*): we would like to speak to the reader's heart.

But the responsibility of the text's author is still greater; one should not write about what one has not experienced. On the other hand, a certain modesty requires the author to adorn his or her experience in poetry or present it in a more or less philosophical prose. In both cases, he or she utilizes words—words, moreover, that die as soon as they are written, like fish taken out of the water. Writing is not the natural element of the word. "The letter kills," Saint Paul says (2 Cor. 3:6); rather, the sheep "hear the voice of the shepherd," Saint John reports (10:27). It is up to the reader not only to read but also to listen to the written word while giving it new life. Let this serve as an excuse for the fact that the pages that follow do not pretend to record experiences but to describe places to which the reader is invited.

Another important remark is necessary. This whole book is an endeavor to liberate God from both specialists and specializations. It is the gospel, the "good news" accessible to children, the humble, the poor—to the people. It is not necessary to belong to a particular caste or to any religion, or even to be a great scholar. But there is one indispensable problem, which is probably the hardest: all the traditions of humanity tell us that those who will be saved, who will be fulfilled, those who will not be reincarnated but arrive at *nirvâna* and attain human plenitude, will be few. We meet God everywhere but not in just any way. We should never make the experience of God banal. Aesthetic ecstasy, erotic rapture, intellectual admiration, biological joy, suffering, or enthusiasm about nature—none of these can be said to be experiences of the divine. They could be so in extreme circumstances, but they would then have to be pure experiences. That is the condition: purity of heart.

I repeat: "Blessed are the pure of heart for they will see God" (Mt. 5:8), they will experience God. A pure heart is an empty heart, without ego, capable of reaching that depth at which the divine lives. The fact that the experience is simple does not mean that it is easy. A text of the *Upanishads,* on which we will comment later on, after having told us that God is found in nourishment, in what is seen, what is heard and understood, adds that in every case mentioned the way passes through asceticism, effort, ardor, *tapas*—purification.

Among the innumerable places where God is to be found, we will briefly mention nine, without explaining precisely what is found in any of them. Don't we all admit that, ultimately, God is ineffable?

## Love

There seems to be unanimity, both in the cultures of the north and of the south, that the most privileged place for the meeting of humans and God is the experience of love. "God is love," and those who encounter love encounter God. Up to this point, there is a great agreement of opinion. The difficulty appears with the dualism in the interior of love itself—ultimately between the world and God.

The relegation of God to a sphere of transcendence and the absolute has created a virtually lethal split in the very being of humans. Love, as the *Vedas* say (*Rigveda* X, 129, 4), has existed from the beginning; it is more sublime than all the gods and is the first seed of the intellect. Humanity's most ancient monuments affirm something quite similar. There is no doubt that love is only another name for the dynamism of every being who tends to that which is not an *aliud* but an *alter:* such is the dynamism of love. We would not be able to experience the desire for God or the aspiration to the divine if that was absolutely foreign and unknown to us. This dynamism demonstrates its validity in everything from the Trinity to the last elementary particle of matter. How could it fail to be a place where one would meet God?

Whatever distinction we might make, in the last instance there is *one and only one love.* In terms of medieval scholasticism, whether Jewish, Christian or Muslim, this ultimate love is God. To the degree that every being desires something, it desires God, as Saint Thomas says explicitly.

Since the heart is the symbol of love, those who have a pure heart will see God. *Ubi caritas et amor, Deus ibi est,* as is prayed in a popular, paraliturgical Christian song.

The mysticism of every age and on every continent has left us pearls of wisdom on the subject of love. "I am the religion of love," says a great mystic of Murcie in the twelfth and thirteenth centuries, and adds, "Where the camels of love are headed is where my religion and faith is found." The heart (*qalb*) is a fundamental idea in Sufism.

The heart, the nearly universal symbol of love, is a human organ that as such affirms the unity of love. "It is through the heart that we know the truth," says another sacred text (*Brihadâranyak Upanishad* III. 9, 23).

*Love is one,* we have said, in a unity that is non-dualistic. There are not two loves, nor can divine and human love be separated, even though one ought to distinguish between them. As soon as this distinction is transformed into a split, however, the rupture constitutes a sin.

It is difficult to enjoy the experience of God's love if one underestimates human love. Similarly, it is difficult to persevere in human love if one doesn't discover in it a divine soul, so to speak. Genuine love is far more than a voluntarist projection or an example of simple sentimentality. It is not a matter of going beyond the love of creatures, of abandoning them in order to raise oneself to the divine love. God does not live only on the mountains of nothingness; God also has a dwelling place in the "wooded valleys" of humanity. It is in human love itself that Divinity resides. As the gospel reminds us, a divine love that is not incarnated in the love of neighbor is nothing but a lie (1 John 4:20).

## The Thou

The love of God and the love of things derive from the same dynamism of our being—what the scholastics would call "appetite." These two loves are distinct but inseparable. It is in the love of neighbor that this non-dualist relationship appears most clearly—in the love of *thou,* our thou. The primacy accorded to the principle of noncontradiction, which is valid in logic but not necessarily in reality, has too frequently led us to divide all of reality in terms of that dualist principle: Christians/non-Christians, believers/nonbelievers, English/non-English, good/bad (the latter being equivalent to those who are not good), and so on. German idealism speaks of *Ich/Nicht Ich* and European Cartesianism similarly starts out from the duality of body/soul, spirit/matter, in which one thing is defined by the fact of not being the other.

The thou is neither the I nor the non-I. Nor is it a middle term that would then permit a synthesis. Its relation is *advaita*; there is no thou without an I and vice versa. The two are correlative.

In human loves the love of thou dominates. This thou is perhaps the most important and most universal place for the experience of God. Indeed, to meet God in one's neighbor is part of the common cultural patrimony of humanity. But we will restrict ourselves here to the experience of God as the experience of thou. Let us recall that, in practice, the wisdom of every people teaches us how openness to the experience of God is able to emerge:

• By means of *knowledge* (*jnâna*): through the effort of the intelligence to transcend itself: God is seen as an I.

• By means of *love* (*bhakti*): through the heart's desire to seek what can fill it: God is seen as a thou.

• By means of *deeds* (*karma*): through the creativity of the creature who wishes to imitate the creator by creating—that is, by doing: God is seen as a he or she (the model, the artist).

The different schools of spirituality that follow one of these three ways are well known. Inasmuch as they are genuine ways, they lead with certainty to God. Our commentary will not limit itself to paths; it will also look at the underlying experience of those who follow them. The first way leads us to God as the ultimate and supreme I: Yahweh, *Aham,* the ultimate subject. "How can we get to know the one who knows?" one *Upanishad* asks. One who knows the I as such cannot be known.

In fact, if we should know that which knows (I, the *subject*), we would transform it into a known *object.* Although we are able to say that the two are the same, our experience will turn on what is known, and not on that which knows. The latter, to the degree that he or she is the one who knows, truly knows; but he or she is not known. In that sense, there is no possible experience of the I. The Son is the one who knows the Father; it is Ishvara who knows itself Brahman, the pure consciousness is pure consciousness and not the consciousness of anything (not even itself); light remains invisible unless what is not light is illuminated. Our experience of the I is an experience of *mine;* it is my experience of the I. But the mine is, while the I is not. The structure of experience thus cannot be monist: it would not have the polarity necessary for every experience. The very structure of experience is non-dualist. It implies a negation of duality without falling into a monolithic monism. Strictly speaking, my I is a thou-I; it is the I of a thou. It is only when I have the experience of I as *yours* that I am able to enter, as a thou, into the experience of I.

In other words, God does not have the experience of "myself." God has it rather of "himself," which precisely implies non-duality, or the Trinity. Brahman does not know that he is Brahman, the Vedanta says. But Ishvara knows it; he knows himself as Brahman. And it is this consciousness of himself as Ishvara that makes Ishvara equal to Brahman.

The way of love discovers God as a thou. The majority of Abrahamic spiritualities see it in this way. God is the thou to whom all prayers are addressed. Nevertheless, strictly speaking, we cannot say that we have the experience of God as a thou. The experience is personal and the thou is thou; I am not me. And "I" ought to be the subject of the experience.

But I am able to experience God while experiencing myself as a thou of God, as I discover myself to be God's—that is to say, when I feel that I am yours. I discover God not when I discover him as a thou to whom I address myself, but as an I who addresses himself to me and of whom my I is the thou. I am then a thou of God. The experience of God, therefore, is the experience of thou, a thou that God calls "thou," the experience that I am precisely "I," my true ego, the self, a thou of God.

The experience of God is so personal because each one of us—all of us—are only that very experience of God in me, in which I discover myself precisely as the thou of that I who names me, and in naming me gives me being, as the texts of both Old and New Testament assert: "Thou art." This discovery is a revelation. God is disclosed in the form of thou: "You are my son" (Mark 1:11; Luke 3:22); "I, today, have begotten you" (Ps. 2:7; Acts 13:33). The initiative comes from me; my I is only a thou, a thou of God. And if I sense that God is saying to me, "Thou art," it is precisely because in truth I am a thou, and God is the *unique* I.

The word with which Jesus blesses Peter is very significant, "Who do people say the Son of Man is?... But you, who do you say I am?" (Matt. 16:13-15). And Peter answers, "Thou art the Christ, the Son of the living God" (Matt. 16:16). Christ blesses Peter because he has pronounced the one word that reveals "thou" to him, "thou art," before he adds, in the language and culture of the time, other predicates and adjectives (messiah, son) as additions to the discovery of thou.

I have defended elsewhere the thesis that the famous affirmation of the *Upanishads*—*tav tvam asi*—does not repeat, like others, "We are Brahman," but that it adds, "Thou art that, Svetaketu, a thou" ("that: thou art"). We are identical with Brahman without ceasing to be what we are, that is, the thou of Brahman, *saguna brahman,* identical with him, *nirguna brahman.* But there is more. Brahman is everything; God is in all things. Consequently, this manner of discovering the divine thou in everything, and especially in our neighbor, is the most common and human way of experiencing God. It is written: "Love your neighbor as yourself." It is only when this "myself" is discovered as a divine thou that we will be able to love the other as a "myself." This is to discover God in one's neighbor, to discover him or her as a thou of God, and hence divine.

We are not talking about a dialectical relationship between the thou and the I but of a non-dualist dialogue. The thou is not the I, but neither is it the non-I. This is what idealism forgets. Between the I and the non-I there is the thou. The thou is thou because it is the thou of the I, and we would be able to affirm the same thing about the subject of I: the I is always an I of a thou. Not even God is a solitary Being, as both Prajâpati and the Trinity, though starting from two different perspectives, remind us. As for us, at the very moment when the I knows itself as thou, that self-same I knows itself as yours, and is therefore saved.

Whoever fails to arrive at the discovery of thou, which obviously cannot be done without thought, without love, and without action, is cut off from the possibility of experiencing the divine. The experience of God is the experience of thou, which leads us to the impossibility of the experience of I alone, precisely because I am not able to experience myself without being "objectivized" in a thou. Hence, when the thou of God is discovered, what we experience is the experience of God making the experience of thou. And as everyone knows, it is only when we love that we discover the thou.

The thou is experienced also in the poor man, the other, and as some will say, the enemy as well: the thou is the leap to a transcendence that never breaks with immanence. Only by starting from the immanence of a thou that discovers itself as "thine" is it possible to experience God. In this way, we return to love, the point of arrival and departure, that love which the *Vedas* say is the first seed of the Spirit (*Atharvaveda* XIX, 52, 1) and the first of the gods (*Atharvaveda* IX, 2, 19), and which Christian Scripture declares is God's self (1 John 4:8 and 16).

"Were I to testify on my own behalf, my testimony would not be valid" (John 5:31). The I does not know itself. In this text Jesus does not say that his testimony would not be valid because it would be a lie. What he says is that he knows that the testimony of a thou whom he calls his Father is genuine. I am not able to know myself and therefore cannot bear a genuine witness to myself. Such a witness ought to be a thou. But this thou is not just anyone whatsoever. It is, rather, my thou that I recognize as such, and for that reason I know and recognize that he tells the truth.

To "know yourself" is therefore possible only if the myself is known by someone who is not just anyone, but is in fact my true *alter*, the thou: I know to the degree to which I am known (1 Cor. 13:12).

This knowledge is at once active and passive. I know inasmuch as I am known, but I also know that I am known. This thou is intimately linked to the I inasmuch as they are neither two nor one: "The depths of a human being can only be known by his or her own spirit, not by any other human" (1 Cor. 2:11). The true thou is the spirit of the human that is within. But the same is true of the depths of God (1 Cor. 2:12). And it is in that Spirit that we are able to experience God. But none of this can be understood without love.

# Joy

Ultimately, all places are linked together. Love is the source of joy, although it can be the source of suffering as well. But perhaps this is appropriate to our time insofar as it "swings" between negative Manichean attitudes toward life and the asphyxiating hedonist situations of life itself.

Max Scheler, in his criticsm of Immanuel Kant and Protestant puritanism, spoke of the "betrayal of joy" by Christianity. But this is not the only example of the absence of joy in religious manifestations. Catholics have been rightly criticized for their "Good Friday" spirituality, a piety that is far removed from life, a spirituality that is virtually the enemy of joy, which is considered as simply a concession to human carnality.

We are not going to stop to recall the scholastic thesis on *beatitudo* in which happiness is seen as the very purpose of our lives. Neither are we going to comment on the *Upanishads* when they describe *ananda,* or happiness, as the essential characteristic of Brahman. We are tempted, however, to cite the *Taittirîya Upanishad* (II, 5, sp.) with its description of Brahman and even *âtman* as happiness.

What is clear is that in the current Western mentality, especially that of the Christian world, joy is not generally seen as one of the places where the experience of God finds one of its purest expressions.

And we say "purest" because, in the experience of joy, reflection plays a minimal and only indirect role. A purely (moral) consciousness is not enough to allow that kind of attenuation of consciousness (intellectual and reflective) that would permit the spontaneity and human joy that the presence of divine realities brings to light. Popular piety with its *gozos* and hymns of praise to the Virgin is sometimes wiser.

"A saint who is sad is a sad saint," Léon Bloy said, and we are familiar with André Gide's criticism of the negative commandments. It hardly seems necessary to quote Albert Camus, Friedrich Nietzsche, and many others, including the verses of Ruben Dario that make the same point—against Thomas à Kempis.

Many have commented in the same style on the usual absence of humor in theology and philosophy.

What we would want to underline here is neither a negative criticism nor a theoretical defense of God as joy, but rather the fact that we do not sufficiently appreciate the fact that it is in joy that we meet God, or that joy is the privileged place for experiencing the divine. We tend to forget that God is the God of the living, and life is *joy*.

We are not stopping to give definitions of joy or make subtle distinctions between happiness, merrymaking, euphoria, satisfaction, felicity, pleasure, enjoyment, jubilation, and numerous other synonyms; what we are attempting to say is more simple. The whole ensemble of synonyms could be reduced to sensation, feeling, and the understanding of life's plenitude. Christ said that he has come to give us life in abundance (John 10:10), and the fundamental text of his message bears the relevant title "The Beatitudes."

It is the part of wisdom to discover true joy and the experience it contains, in which one finds the very source of delight and which comes close to being a definition of God.

It is extremely significant that Christianity, which ought to be understood as the religion of joy, is so frequently considered a sad religion. The alleluias and cries of praise are the most frequent prayers in the Judeo-Christian tradition. Sadness (*acedia*) was long considered a mortal sin. The very word *grace,* not only in Greek but also in English, connotes joy and jubilation. The *gaudium de veritate* (rejoicing in truth) is part and parcel of the most ancient Christian tradition. And the resurrection of the body holds a central place in the Christian message. Nevertheless, the equilibrium has often been lost. Numerous Christians go through life with a guilt complex. And a certain negative spirituality regarding life has invaded many circles that have come to confuse perfection with what is least natural, yet has sometimes been baptized as supernatural.

Perhaps it is the responsibility of contemporary pedagogy to teach the true pleasures of life, those pleasures that are the most fundamental precisely because they are the most elementary. We return again and again to the same point: only the innocent know complete joy and only a pure heart experiences joy—and with it, God.

Perhaps it is opportune here to mention again the text of the *Taittirîya Upanishad* (III, 3.1, sq.), when, speaking of Brahman as happiness, it confirms the idea that the knowledge of Brahman is an encounter with nourishment (food, *annam*), life (breath, *prâna*), intellect (*manas*), and intelligence (*vijnâna*)—that is, with an experience of human activity at its greatest depth,

Here, as everywhere, it is appropriate to maintain a middle way: "Nothing to excess" is an aphorism of the pre-Socratics, in addition to being a tautology.

# Suffering

We ought to distinguish between pain, sorrow, and suffering. All three words are ambiguous and are too often used indiscriminately. Without pretending to define them, I would understand pain as basically a biological sensation. Animals feel pain and a number of authors speak of "soul pain," since animals have a soul. Sorrow would be chiefly a psychophysical pain. Sorrow inflicts itself and is felt in the soul; sometimes the word is used to express something uniquely spiritual. We use the word *suffering* as the combination between the bodily, the psychic, and the spiritual. A certain kind of sadness is not incompatible with joy. Suffering the divine, *Pati divina*, is a traditional phrase of Latin mysticism that includes all the ambivalence of that sentence. If the experience of God in joy is ecstatic, then in suffering it may be called enstatic—to use the word Mircea Eliade has introduced, *enstasis*.

Pain causes suffering, injustice, humiliation, punishment, hunger, the loss of a good, the agony of an endangered and uncertain future. It is not only the words that are ambivalent in this area, but the effects they produce. Suffering is capable of bringing us closer to God, but it also can separate us from the divine. It can purify or degrade us, make us mature, or bring us to despair.

We are not entering here into the area of voluntary sufferings, as practiced by a series of spiritualities of both East and West, which believe that voluntary suffering is capable of purifying us. It is a fact that this belief, shared by many sannyasis, monks, and even mystics, has produced positive results, however absurd they appear to us. Contemporary myth, however, rejects such negative asceticisms.

I would like to discuss here suffering that is not self-inflicted but that is provoked by all kinds of causes, from that produced by an illness affecting us or someone else, to the physical and moral hardships due to unjust situations at the personal or the social level.

The passion for justice leads to suffering when one sees the forces of evil or the simple inertia of history offer resistance and defend themselves by attacking. Recent examples of the persecutions of Christians in Latin America because they wanted to change an unjust *status quo* constitute a clear illustration of this case. The situation of Tibet or of many countries in Africa, to cite only the most obvious examples, cannot leave us indifferent.

Personal suffering is also a meeting place with the divine, although it remains good advice, both psychological and religious, not to take pleasure in suffering as an end in itself. Nevertheless, suffering is a kind of existential awakening to a depth dimension in ourselves as well as in reality as a whole. According to popular wisdom, unhappiness brings us closer to God and to others; no alchemical transformation is needed for suffering to open us to Mystery rather than plunge us into despair.

Suffering is often so inexplicable that it brings us close to the divine mystery itself: it is the arena that reveals our freedom. "Learn to discern Brahma by means of ascesis" (*Tapasa brahma vijijnâsasva*) is the refrain of the *Upanishad* already cited (*Taittirîya* II, 1, sq.). Suffering is closely related to the sensibility that is as much psychosomatic as cosmic, insofar as it entails, in the latter case, participation in solidarity with the universe.

It is obvious that belief in a good and omnipotent God can give rise to blasphemy in us rather than submission to what we cannot but consider as immoral—whether in God's not stopping evil when able or permitting it in view of a higher good, as if the end justified the means. We have here an example of an experience affected by a previous interpretation of God, but perhaps the very experience of suffering purifies the idea of God.

One fact, however, is empirically established: suffering, like joy, is a human situation that can serve both as a vehicle for experiencing God as well as the complete opposite. Suffering confronts us with the irrational, with human wickedness, with evil, with the collapse of all our plans and security. It decenters us and dislocates us, removes every impression we have of being self-sufficient, strips us of everything and places us before what is painful and incomprehensible. It makes us indignant, and we instinctively revolt against it. Think of the suffering of a person condemned to death or to life imprisonment, whether guilty or innocent. Think not just of a Job but of the millions of our brothers and sisters who suffer—suffering to a much greater extent than we ever might be able to relieve. Here the experience of God, before being a consolation, is a communion. We touch grace in the same way that we make contact with mystery.

The spirituality of the bodhisattva is an example that offers hope. The bodhisattva does not lose his joy but remains on earth to participate in the suffering of creatures in order thereby to help them liberate themselves.

We have said that suffering can be an awakening to transcendence and in this way be a meeting place with God. We ought to complete this thought by saying that it can equally be a revelation of immanence—where we also encounter God.

The bodhisattva, the saint, and the wise one suffer not so much by reason of what does them harm individually but perhaps even more for humanity, for all sensible beings, for the cosmos. That is the experience of *buddhakâya*, of *karma*, of the Mystical Body of Christ, of universal solidarity—to give quite different examples of this experience of universal solidarity. The reason that makes those who are "fulfilled" more open to this participation in reality is simple. The *mahatma* (the magnanimous one, the great soul), the *jîvanmukta* (liberated soul), the *insan kamil* (perfect one), the *shen jen* (the holy one), the saint (*hagios, sanctus, kadosh,* etc.), the *edel mensch* (the noble soul, according to Eckhart, commenting on Lk. 19:12), to cite a great diversity of traditions—in a word, those who have reached human plenitude—have broken the barriers of individualism and entered into communion with the entire cosmos. The wise person is the one who captures the hearts of all people. Meister Eckhart, repeating a popular belief, affirms that "he who knows himself knows all creatures" (in his treatise on *The Noble Man*). This linking up of everything with everything else unites us to reality through contemplation, prayer, and glory, as well as by means of participation in the sufferings of creation, whether the agony of childbirth or of despair.

Here is another empirical fact: human beings seem to feel the link that unites them to all of reality when they are more conscious of the negative than the positive aspects—in the same way that we rarely think of our stomach when it functions normally.

In sum, suffering makes us feel our human condition and our creaturely state more profoundly, regardless of how it is interpreted. It is enough to listen to the text of any musical rendering of the *Stabat Mater* of Christian tradition (even if it isn't by Palestrina) to understand what I mean. It is a matter of participation through love in the pain of another. This awareness of being part of a whole opens us to God's hope. The fact is well known: prisoners and victims of human cruelty collapse less readily if they keep alive their faith in something that transcends them and that at the same time lives within them.

Belief in satisfaction by substitution, as well as in a certain usefulness of suffering, can be a great consolation, although the pure experience of the divine mystery is capable of assuming more radical forms that border on the terrible and the horrible. Faith is neither the rationalization of God nor of life. Christ's cry of despair on the cross is instructive. But his last exclamation is also revealing: "Into your hands I commend my spirit" (Luke 23:46). In any case, we should recognize that the experience of God is no trifling affair.

## Evil

This section may shock those who hold an excessively unilateral idea of divine reality. We credit God with everything that is good and positive, while we forget that "the Gods love obscurity" (*Aitareya Upanishad* I, 3, 14) and that a number of them are beyond good and evil (and hence take no part in human quarrels). We also believe that even the God of the gospel makes the sun shine on both the just and the impious, and that it rains on both the good and the evil. The question is indeed delicate. We do not say that God is in any way "bad": we content ourselves with noting that we also encounter God in the experience of evil.

We understand that a certain Christian puritanism is scandalized by the affirmation that evil is a privileged place for experiencing God. This "scandal" arises from dualist thought, which allows no place for evil inasmuch as it absolutizes that self-same evil. Nevertheless, in Christian tradition itself, the paschal liturgy in its canticle of glory has not censured the famous passage regarding the *felix culpa*; original sin is seen as a "happy fault" that has brought us such a glorious redeemer.

This profound intuition of contemplative liturgy liberates us from the purely dialectical thinking that has dominated the West in these last centuries. In effect, by virtue of the fact that sin is not virtue, dialectical thinking is capable of "justifying" sin (in this case, that of Adam and Eve) only by defending the immoral theory that the one who wishes the end also wishes the means.

If original sin was a *felix culpa*, according to such thinking, the reason is this: it is justified by having been the "means" of redemption. In this way everything is justified eschatologically. Insofar as it is *culpa*, it cannot be *felix*, and therefore we cannot glorify it. If evil is the non-good, we cannot in any way encounter God in it, nor can we pretend that the sin is a "fortunate sin"—that is, justify it by its consequences (redemption). Neither is it comprehensible, according to the current theology of redemption, that God permitted—and even, perhaps, decreed—the crucifixion of his Son for the sake of a greater good. From such a position, it is just a step to defend not only the Crusades and the Inquisition, but also the "just war" and savage capitalism (for the benefit of the victims, although always delayed until much later).

By affirming here that evil can be the place for meeting the supreme good, however, we are saying that evil is neither absolute nor absolutely opposed to the good; obviously, it is not dialectically contradictory to the good.

The experience of evil, therefore, confronts us with our weakness, with our own sin. We cannot deny that wickedness is real, and so we recognize it as such. Our recognition of evil is a good, a good *sui generis*. Is it not a daily experience to observe that those who have not known evil are, shall we say, almost inhuman? The publican in the Gospel and the elder son in the parable of the prodigal son are two notorious examples. "For the one who has loved much, much will be pardoned" is another evangelical *koan*.

Religion includes what is best in human beings. It is from religious inspiration that many of the greatest geniuses and works of art (for example, the cathedrals, the most sublime temples) have emerged. Heroic acts have been performed in its name. But religion has also produced what is worst, what is most wicked. Religion has not only been an opiate but a poison as well, and it has served as excuse for committing the greatest crimes and causing the worst aberrations. Evil is an integral part of reality and of religion, precisely because it is real and thereby participates in this ambivalence.

**A Fact.** Without entering now into long metaphysical discussions, the problem of evil is definitely a fact as well as an intrinsically religious question that has stimulated humanity, throughout its entire history, to try to explain it by proposing the most diverse theories. From the conception of evil as being no more than an appearance, to the recognition of evil's reality as equal to the principle of the good, we find a range of hypotheses that correspond to the various visions of the world. It is interesting to recognize, too, that the great religions are not centered on humanity but on the cosmos, in whose development evil plays an active role. It is well to remember the numerous cosmogonies in which evil seems to be original sin, the origin of the actual condition of the cosmos.

**Unintelligible.** Evil as evil is unintelligible. The *mysterium iniquitatis* (mystery of evil) is a mystery precisely because our reason cannot grasp it. Besides, we find neither an explanation for it nor any internal intelligibility; it has proved incomprehensible for us. If we did succeed in explaining evil, if through Sigmund Freud, Carl Jung, or Jacques Lacan we found the key that permitted us to justify it, then evil would no longer exist. If we were indeed capable of explaining it, our discovery would only be a bomb whose detonator should immediately be turned off: it would then be deactivated. Once the mystery was deactivated, evil would no longer exist.

Evil exhibits no internal intelligibility; it commands no ultimately rational explanation. There is no reason capable of explaining it because it would then cease to be evil. If it were grounded in a sufficient reason, it would be merely reasonable. There cannot be evil for an omniscient being. In fact, no absolute monotheism will grant any metaphysical consistency to evil. To search for a cause of evil leads back to an ultimate cause, which would then challenge the principle of the Good, as all cosmological dualisms have observed. In the opposite case, Satan (as symbol of evil) still continues to be a faithful collaborator of God, as we see him, pathetically, in the book of Job. *Von Zeit zu Zeit seh ich dens Alten gern* ("I like to go see the Ancient One from time to time"), Mephistopheles tells us in *Faust*.

But the *mysterium iniquitatis* also constitutes a moral challenge to monotheism: how can evil exist in a radical monotheism that believes in a good and all-powerful God? The Jewish Kabbalah, which offers the hypothesis of a God who withdraws, would illustrate a further attempt at an explanation. Another example, drawn from Islamic theology—which perhaps represents the purest monotheism (and is not inclined to reduce evil to nothing but a pure appearance)—can serve to show how, in the ultimate instance, evil is in fact an integral part of the divine plan.

Let me summarize the pathetic and moving story of the *Kitāb al-Ṭawāsīn*, attributed to the great mystic martyr Al-Hallāj, which was translated by Louis Massignon. According to a variety of texts, Iblīs (Lucifer), the most beautiful of the angels, the first and most glorious of the creatures that sprang forth from the hands of the Creator, challenges God when the latter lets him know that he will have to serve, and even adore, a mortal being composed of flesh and mud, the human. Iblīs refuses and says: "I am the one who knows you best of all; I am your most perfect creature. I have sworn fidelity and eternal love to you. How can you want me to turn my back on you who are the light and source of all, and go to serve—even if it is you who gives the orders—another creature who is distinct from you?" He knows that God intends to put into motion time and creation, and he has decided to disobey out of love and fidelity while accepting the responsibility and punishment for his act. Iblīs is blinded by love and reacts like a lover.

One day Moses and Iblīs meet, and Moses asks, "What prevented you from prostrating yourself?" To which Iblīs responds that it is precisely his vision of God as the only one to be adored that has prevented it, "while you have turned your back on Him by going to the mountain."

"Haven't you thereby transgressed a divine commandment?" Moses asks. "It was not a commandment," Satan answers, "it was only a test." "Are you sinless, then?" Moses asks again. And Iblīs reiterates his love and fidelity to God, arguing that if God had truly loved him, Iblīs would not have had any other option than to obey him; but since he does not obey God, it means that God needs him in his plans.

"Then you remember him?" asks Moses. "Oh, Moses," he responds. "Pure thought has no need of recollection...His memory and mine will never be able to be separated...And I serve him with a greater purity, a more glorious recollection. Before, I served him for my joy; now I serve him for his."

God and Iblīs—theirs is the story of an incomprehensible fidelity, if we do not understand what love and fidelity are. The experience of evil cannot be separated from the existence of a living God, precisely because God is all of reality. The ultimate explanation would perhaps be this greater fidelity to what makes possible the launching of the mystery of time.

In a nonmonotheistic perspective, there is not such repugnance to integrating evil within the very bosom of divinity. Indra, for example, the great Vedic god, Lord of good and evil, commits acts that, from an ethical viewpoint, are in many ways immoral. Indra lies, deceives, makes use of good and evil as it seems good to him, throws everything upside down. Unlike the Christian mentality, in which God is incapable of doing evil, divinity is able to prompt evil, and in this way prompt us to experience God in the very experience of evil.

But the theology of Indra goes even further. Indra is not only what is represented by his popular epithet, *Indra Vritahan*, "he who, in killing him, is conqueror of the demon Vrita," he who provokes a deadly dryness by holding back the imprisoned waters: Indra is beyond good and evil. As the *Upanishad* says regarding a perfect man, he never torments himself by asking whether he has done good or evil (*Brihadaranyaka* IV, 4, 22; *Tait.* U. II, 9, 2). The great book of Hindu wisdom, the *Mahâbhârata* (XII, 337-340), puts this counsel in the mouth of someone who has achieved fulfillment: "Renounce both good and evil; renounce both the truth and the lie; and, having renounced them, renounce (the consciousness) of that very renunciation." Bringing water to our mill (for we are unable to consider the whole problematic), unlike Plato we will say that the experience of God is not necessarily or altogether to be seen as the experience of the Good.

Tell me what you see "beyond good and evil," Naciketas demands to Yama, the God of the other world (*Kath.* U. I, 2, 14). Notice that the texts cited tell us clearly that we cannot be beyond good unless we are simultaneously beyond evil. If God is, at the very least, the epitome of all reality, then the experience of God puts us in contact not only with the highest heavens but also "with the depths of Satan" (Ap II, 24); the Vulgate ironically translates this as "the heights of Satan."

**Linked to the experience of God.** We say that the experience of evil is intimately linked to the experience of God for two reasons.

The first is that, without in any way denying morality and ethics (if one is able to distinguish them), the experience of God transcends both. Religion is not simply ethics, even though we probably cannot separate them. To say this in the language of tradition: the divine mystery is beyond good and evil. In saying that it transcends this dualism we are by no means absolutely affirming that this is a good—or an evil.

The second reason is more delicate. We have said that evil is an uncontested fact, a reality that we can neither deny nor evade. We have also said that evil is unintelligible, which leads us to discover the revelatory character of evil. What evil reveals to us is that there *is* something unintelligible, that reality does not reduce to rationality or intelligibility. And this opens up a radical metaphysical option. The following are the alternatives.

First, evil might be incomprehensible for human intelligence, but not for divine omniscience. Then God would know evil, but therefore would no longer be God. On this option, for God, there would be no evil: torture, hatred, injustice would not, strictly speaking, be evil; the fact is that we simply are myopic. If God permits it, there must be a reason. We are in the habit of saying so, and we console ourselves by our belief that we are dealing with an enigma, which we may resolve in another life. Monotheism encourages such a solution.

We must point out here, just the same, a philosophical a priori to this position: that reality is intelligible. An omniscient God, in fact, is that being who knows everything, and so by that very fact becomes knowable. The omniscient Being knows everything knowable, but not necessarily all of reality, unless we identify reality with the capacity of being known.

This brings us to the second option of the alternatives. On this understanding, evil is real. It is the obscure part of reality, its unintelligible aspect. In the adventure of the real, God would be co-implicated like ourselves who, in the words of

Saint Paul, are God's cooperators, although not equally nor on the same level. It is on this side that the cosmotheandric adventure is situated. But that is perhaps enough for our purposes here.

Insofar as it concerns us, then, we may conclude that to attack the problem of evil necessarily implicates our experience of God. And perhaps the kind of God we have been talking about teaches us what is most practical and necessary, without metaphysical encumbrances: to confront ourselves with the problem of evil without any ulterior motive.

**Innocence.** There is no way of eliminating evil by making use of a counter-evil; *reconciliation* is the one effective way of overcoming evil. By itself, dialectical confrontation only leads to a truce . . . until the vanquished take their revenge. Evil is impermeable to reason, and because of that fact, to judgment. It is written that we must not judge (Matt. 7:1), especially interiorly.

Reason neither assuages evil nor eliminates evil. The Christian liturgy opposes the Stoic ideal of living according to reason (*vivere secundum rationem*) with living in the love of God (*vivere secundum te*). Evil can be transformed only by the heart. Reason by itself can press us to perform reasonable acts. Not even a pure heart can do this, though this statement, like all fruitful tautologies, is a qualified one. Innocence, that forgotten beatitude (Matt. 5:5), is that "which will possess the earth," not that which will achieve victory over evil. Creation must not be destroyed.

We have made this digression in order to remove two illusions from those who imagine the experience of God as a bed of flowers for privileged souls who have never known evil. In spite of the romantic summaries found in the "lives of the saints," it is they themselves who tell us that they are great sinners. Leaving aside psychology, we say that it is the experience of evil that most often stimulates and introduces us to the experience of God—and may indeed constitute part of the same experience. A real God—a God who is not just a pure idea—cannot be ignorant of the existence of evil. Jesus Christ, to all appearances, did experience evil and, even, abandonment by God. It is possible that reality exhibits an opaque facet through which the God of monotheism simply cannot enter. The problems are terribly serious, and our technocratic superficiality is little accustomed to them, despite the multiple manifestations of evil in our time. "It is fearful to fall into the hands of the living God," Saint Paul exclaims. Human existence is not a frivolous game for children. We should leave the question there in order to proceed to a special example that is a little less tragic.

**Transgression.** One way of being open to transcendence— of going beyond our own limits, of catching a glimpse of the infinite and the unknown—is, precisely, *transgression.* When someone has contravened a norm he or she considers obligatory, the rupture suffered is so great, and the world into which he or she has penetrated so strange and dangerous, that pardon or despair are the only alternatives that do not cheapen the irreversible transgression. When we transgress, we eliminate any possibility of going back, of piecing together what we have broken. In the necessity of overcoming this agony, of moving beyond the evil committed, we find an opening to transcendence: a conscious and responsible transcendence. If we reduce it to an everyday matter, however, we no longer are dealing with transgression but rather a simple, trivial *faux pas.* The anonymous woman who anointed Jesus' feet (Luke

1:36-50) loved deeply precisely because she had been greatly pardoned, and she was greatly pardoned precisely because she loved so much. This is a vital circle, a circle that vibrates with life. It is not a vicious circle, like those that reason generates.

Transgression confronts us in our freedom, and therefore entails our responsibility. Jesus' initially disconcerting phrase has not been accepted as canonical and hence does not appear in the Vulgate, though it is found in numerous important Greek texts and is not apocryphal. The phrase refers to the Sabbath. As he is passing through the Galilean countryside, Jesus meets a man who is working on the Sabbath and says to him, "O man, blessed are you," if you know what you are doing (in breaking the Sabbath and having the courage to do so; blessed are you if you transgress while knowing that you transgress). But if you do not know this, then you are accursed and a lawbreaker (Luke 6:4). This is the exact opposite of the morality of the confessional. In the latter morality, a non-culpable ignorance liberates us from sin. But that morality does not result from this passage, one worth comparing with Jesus' iconoclastic affirmation that the Sabbath is made for man and not man for the Sabbath. This text is certainly dangerous and destabilizing. Socrates was condemned on the pretext that he was corrupting youth, Al Hallāj and many others because they uttered a blasphemy or defended a heresy, Jesus because he claimed to renew the Law while going beyond it and establishing freedom. It is not uniquely the Sanhedrin but the Vatican too— and many other institutions—that have been and remain "prudent." "The truth will make you free" (John 8:32)—true, but freedom *is* dangerous. Reason is often on the side of Torquemada; to contradict it means risking the cross. But man is not reason alone.

We are not saying, *Pecca fortiter*—sin boldly. It is not a matter of defending sin or anarchy. Let us restrict ourselves to our case. The experience of transgression, even simply on a psychological level, encourages an opening to a "more," introduces a readiness for change, for new beginnings, and transforms the person. In the prototype of the perfect saint, who never has sinned, never fallen, never committed evil, this experience of fallibility, of contingency, is clearly lacking. Absent is the pain in his own flesh, the pain without which comprehension and the acceptance of the human condition are very difficult. Without that pain, love is impossible. Unlike mercy and compassion, love is an equalizing, communitarian link. We cannot love from on high; we must find ourselves on the same level. As a consequence, the one who loves is vulnerable. Without the *kenosis* of Jesus Christ, his "redemption" by means of love remains incomprehensible. "For our sake God made the sinless one into sin" (2 Cor. 5:21), declares a bold text of Paul. *O felix culpa* (O happy fault) sings the liturgy.

Christian scholasticism passionately discussed the following question: Would Christ have become incarnate had humanity not sinned? Responding in the affirmative, Duns Scotus always has been more convincing to me than Saint Thomas, who supported the negative. Christ is not merely the one who comes to cure a wound or restore an order disrupted by sin, but is the one who leads creation to its culminating point, its divine purpose. Still, all these suppositions are but wild imaginings, for the situation of humanity and the cosmos, as it emerges from the creative or permissive hands of God, is one of disharmony—in traditional terms, original sin. If it is a flight from the real world to the heaven of a disincarnate God, it cannot be an experience of the real God. The Christian experience of the divine mystery, inseparable as it is from a divine incarnation, cannot be linked with docetist descent (like an *avantâra*) but emerges from an event in the very bosom of the Trinity and history. Hence the Christian experience of God also includes the experience of evil. This is not just the experience of *an idea* but of the dimension of reality we usually call God and which, according to Christian faith, is incarnated at the heart of the cosmos itself. The distinction between Christ and Jesus already is explained.

Meditation on evil, which transcends disobedience and transgression, including the sense of sin, introduces us to a new aspect of the experience of God, an aspect that entails a revelation from reality. The problem of evil breaks the schemas we have made about God a priori, disrupts our categories, and makes us understand that we do not have an answer for everything. It makes us humble and more realistic. It should help us realize there is not only the community of saints but also the community of sinners. It makes us understand that the passion of Christ is also the passion of God.

## Pardon

The vast majority of modern theological dictionaries omit the word *pardon*. When some do speak of it, they rarely move beyond its juridical, moral, or liturgically sacramental aspect. They fall into the habit of interpreting it as a renunciation of the demand for "merited" punishment for a crime or an offense. As an act of generosity, it does not get us closer to God. But here we are referring to something more fundamental.

Nor will we return to theological considerations of pardon as an act of "de-creation"—that is, a human act that cancels what it pardons. We limit ourselves to the experience of meeting with God in and through the act of pardoning. By pardon we understand something more than the act of excusing a debt, of not demanding the practice of retributive justice, or being satisfied with a juridical reconciliation. Reconciliation is generally reciprocal, although it is found on different levels. Pardon is something more: an active action requiring reciprocity—although it can provoke the latter by beginning with a unilateral initiative.

A passage in Saint John's Gospel (20:22-23) connects the reception of the Holy Spirit with the ability to pardon. In fact, those who pardon feel they are doing so not by virtue of a syllogism nor through the reasoning of common sense (proving that, without pardon, we do evil to ourselves and others). The act of pardoning lies beyond the domain of will. I might forego the demand for satisfaction, abandon the urge to punish, no longer wish evil to the one who has offended me, and even forget the offense. But something would still be lacking: the Holy Spirit. The Spirit is a force given to me, something not from myself, something that liberates me just as it liberates the "sinner." The Jewish people already realized that God and only God can pardon.

We insist: pardon is neither a mutual reconciliation, a nonaggresion pact, nor a renunciation of vengeance—the experience of pardon belongs on another level. In the first place, we feel our powerlessness, for we would sometimes like to pardon but cannot do so. So we neither return evil for evil nor seek revenge. But to pardon, however, belongs to an ontologically different level. It is something we experience as a grace, an act we feel ourselves incapable of but that will one fine day become possible.

The absence of pardon is what overloads the negative *karma* in the history of a humanity that, while dreaming of a victory of good over evil, proceeds from vengeance to vengeance, from reparation to counterreparation, from war to war. If we do not pardon a Hitler, for example, the evil he represents will reappear in other dictators and monsters who succeed in obtaining supreme power, whether military, economic, or religious.

Someone who has been capable of pardoning has certainly encountered God. The experience of pardon shatters all our plans, those of the intelligence and those of the will. It is impossible for the intelligence not to know that someone has done me an irreparable injury. It is impossible for the will not to want "justice" done and the debt settled. And if I pardon, it is neither because I believe my act will be useful (who knows if it will be beneficial?) nor because I want to pardon (in order to be good or zealous). Rather, when I pardon genuinely, I do so in a spontaneous and free way, without thinking of either motive or consequence. From the very depth of my being, something or someone has given me the strength to pardon. The Spirit (divine) has acted in and through me.

## Crucial Moments

Time is not homogeneous, nor is life an indifferent succession of events. In the life of every human being we discover some special moments as well as others that weigh heavily on one's life. Birth, death, initiation, marriage, illness, a meeting, a love, the dazzling discovery of an aesthetic or intellectual experience—as well as many other events in human life—awaken us to a dimension that often seems to have been slumbering in the very depth of our being. We did not imagine that we were capable of living with such intensity and depth.

It is often a question of an experience of a religious type. At other times, what we experience does not seem in accord with what people call God nor with what is called religion. We tend to think that these experiences, apparently so different from what we ordinarily think of as "religious," are just as authentic as those generally considered as such. Whether festive or filled with grief, these moments are occasions of celebration: the festival is the natural time for a meeting with the numinous.

We cannot shut God up in a temple, even though we need not, for that reason, become the kind of iconoclasts who render judgment regarding the precise place in which the divine ought or ought not to fix its residence. We ourselves are temples of the Holy Spirit.

What we call the "sanctification of feasts"—all religions celebrate holy days—cannot be reduced to the atavism that prohibits "servile work," a practice that was established in earlier times to protect the poor. Such sanctification reminds us that God is the God of festival and that celebration is a privileged place for meeting God.

We have spoken of joy. The festival underlines the communitarian character of joy, participation, and the interchange between three worlds—the material, the human, and the divine.

These moments I call crucial because they reveal to us a crossroad in our lives. They constitute moments of discontinuity, and therefore place us, in an existential manner, before what certain scholastics have called "continuous creation." Buddhists too affirm the constant recreation of everything. The idea has developed in both traditions because, in a sense, permanent substance does not exist. The Gospels themselves speak not only of a new heaven but also of a new earth—in a passage that is not necessarily eschatological. Novelty and perpetual surprise are phenomenological traits of God. Were I not afraid of being too paradoxical I would say that the readiness to be surprised and to wonder is almost a requirement for experiencing God—who, we should note, does not permit himself to be imprisoned in either physical or metaphysical forms. The God of the past is nothing but a simple "construction" of the mind; it is *not* the "living God."

Between these moments death is dominant in all its aspects, and undeniably the point at which we encounter its mystery. Although we are incapable of a personal experience of death, we can experience the death of others, particularly those we love. This love liberates us from an individualistic prison: the death of a person we love suggests that our self ends neither with our body nor our individuality. We cannot, of course, experience the death of the other, but we can, and do, experience something that, at the time, also dies in us, something that belongs to us. Inasmuch as the subject of our experience continues to live, we surely enjoy a full and lucid consciousness of it. We are not saying that the mysterious, the ineffable, the incomprehensible, is in itself identical to the experience of God, but that it is a privileged locus of that experience.

But there is more, because death is not a simple physiological experience. The death of the self, spoken of in virtually all the world's spiritualities, is very real. The *jīvanmukta,* the risen one, the one confirmed in grace, who has reached fulfillment, who is dead to the old self or has overcome his or her egoism, is ready for the experience of God. One must become "nothing" to experience the Creator of nothingness.

In thinking of crucial moments, we are not thinking only of what Stefan Zweig called the stellar moments of humanity—that is, the events that took place at Sinai, at the Jordan, at Bhudgaya, at Vrindabana, or of other acts of historic transcendence, whether social or personal. We are also thinking of those moments that I will call "interstitials," which exist without any apparent transcendence, whether social or personal. These are small, humble moments that flow, it seems, between two acts of life that apparently are much less important: we have missed a train, the mail does not come, a visit is late, a coffee taken in haste is too hot, or we arrive late for a rendezvous. We are in the process of "wasting time"—it is as if the divine dimension of reality were hidden in this one small unimportant fact. It is written that God is a hidden being, whose tabernacle is found in the shadows and whose recreation consists in chatting with people, even about cooking and sex. Neither a fall from a horse nor an encounter with an angel is required: sometimes, all that is needed is a misstep on the street in order to find "the God of little things." Sometimes God takes us without warning and at other times supplies us with energy and inspiration. The reign of God does not arrive with great fanfare; neither the bridegroom nor the thief arrives at the anticipated hour. Additional explanations are perhaps unneeded. Some schools of spirituality have called this kind of experience "the practice of the presence of God."

## Nature

The absence of an *advaita* experience (even though it is the key to a philosophical vision of the Trinity) has led Christianity to allow itself to be invaded by a panic fear of a so-called pantheism. To avoid monism, Christians fall into dualism. God and the world are radically separated, which means that the transcendent God becomes progressively more superfluous, relegated to a heaven that is not even the heaven of the astronomers. Not only did the Creator rest on the seventh day, but it seems that he also retreated into a celestial vault and thus ceased to create, while at the same time leaving himself connected to an evolutionary "superautomatism."

Although humans become so in community, the human community is not limited to its fellow human creatures. The human community is also cosmic, since the human being is an integral and, even, constitutive part of the cosmos.

Nature is one of the places in which the average person is capable of the most profound encounter with the divine mystery. Our contact with nature is not primarily conceptual but, rather, existential, even cutaneous, a characteristic that does not eliminate the participation of our intellect in the experience of nature.

In saying *nature* we are thinking of everything that is natural, not restricting ourselves to a refined and perhaps artificial vision. And this leads us to an idea that underlies this whole chapter. For humans, the experience of God, not paradoxically but naturally, is quite obvious and, of course, natural. Saint Thomas in his *Summa theologiae* (I, q. 60, a. I, ad 3) even goes so far as to say that the knowledge, delight, and natural inclinations (*cognitio, dilectio,* and *inclinatio naturales*) are always true and accurate. Otherwise we would withdraw all trust (*derogari*) in the author of nature.

While nature as the temple of God is a well-known image, it usually is interpreted in a way that keeps divine transcendence intact, at the price of forgetting God's immanence. Everything pantheism affirms on the positive side is perfectly acceptable; its error consists only in omission and not excess. All is divine, but the divine is not exhausted in what we call reality. A better metaphor is the one certain religious traditions have developed: the world is the body of God, not understood as a Cartesian separation but as a positive symbiosis, one that does not eliminate differences but overcomes separation.

The experience of the divine in nature is not reducible to an earthly numinous feeling regarding a *mysterium fascinans et tremens.* The relationship is a great deal more intimate: it is not a matter of performing a pirouette in order to leap to a first efficient cause that is separate and separable from what is caused. "Creation" is inseparable from the "Creator": if the "Creator" stopped creating even for a second, creation would return to the nothingness from which it proceeded. By means of causality, the intellect is capable of ascending even to God, but a person is not simply intellect; his or her relation to God is immediate and therefore does not require the mediation of reason.

Nature is not only a privileged but also a natural place for meeting God. It is an experience capable of assuming several forms and one that has been the object of innumerable interpretations.

The experience of God in nature is not primarily the experience of the one who makes it, whether creator or artist.

Nor is it the experience of another force that sustains or gives existence to what we call the natural order. It is not what our aesthetic sense or calculation discovers, what the microscope, the telescope, or even rational thought may reveal. It is not a question of raising ourselves to the level of nature's author or penetrating the mysterious depths of the cosmos. It is primarily an experience both more simple and more profound, not an experience of either immanence or transcendence, nor an experience of an Other, but the experience of a Presence, of the more real presence of the actual thing in itself, from which we are not absent. To repeat, the experience of God is the total experience of the human being, in which nature is not absent.

## Silence

As we said earlier, silence is an indispensable condition for preventing our discourse about God from degenerating into sheer verbosity. I insist once again that silence is not only the condition but also the atmosphere in which the experience of God can breath without getting drowned in dialectics.

While apophatic theology often seems frightening, it nevertheless directs our attention to contemplation. Knowing how to listen is the gate to contemplation, especially if we remain aware that the highest knowledge is *not* to know and that every time we name God—every time we conceptualize God—we commit a profanation, a blasphemy.

Some verses of Angelus Silesius exhort us not to leave the sphere of silence in order to arrive at the experience of God, inasmuch as God is silence itself. The following lines are part of this author's only known work, *Der cherubinische Wandersmann*

(*The Cherubic Pilgrim*), and we translate them freely:

*Gott ist so über all's, dass man nicht sprechen kann,*
*Drum betest du ihn auch mit Schweigen an.* (I, 240)
God is so far beyond everything that we can scarcely speak,
Thus it is also by means of your silence that you adore him.

*Schweig, Alleliebster, schweig: kannst du nur gänzlich schweigen,*
*Si wird dir Gott mehr Gut's, als du begehrst, erzeigen.* (II, 8)
Remain silent, beloved, silent: if you can rest completely
in silence,
Then God will give you more blessings than you
would know how to ask for.

*Mensch, so du willst das Sein der Ewigheit aussprechen,*
*So musst du dich zuvor des Redens ganz entbrechen.*
If you wish to express the being of eternity,
You first must abandon all discourse.

*Wenn du an Gott gedenkst, so hörst du ihm in dir,*
*Schweigst du und wärest still, er red'te für und für.* (V, 330)
When you remember God, you hear him in yourself.
You become quiet and if you remain silent and peaceful,
he will not stop speaking to you.

*Niemand red't weniger als Gott ohne Zeit und Ort:*
*Er spricht von Ewigkeit nur bloss, ein einzig Wort.* (IV, 129)
No one speaks less than God, without time or place.
From all eternity he utters only a single word.

God's unique way of speaking is in the vocative; the nominative does not exist, and all other cases are but anthromorphism and idolatry. The vocative is the exclamation that bursts from the depths of the soul, from such inner depths that it is even in danger of not being heard by the one who is calling out. Only when the left hand does not know what the right hand is doing is the action of the right hand authentic (Matt. 6:3). Only when prayer bursts from the depths of my soul and remains in the secret chamber of my being, is that prayer genuine (Matt. 6:5ff.). If it is simply a matter of loving our friends, Christ says, the pagans do that already (Matt. 5:47; 6:32): they pray, sing hymns, love, and chant, but none of all that reaches God. These are only approximations, gestures that are successful if performed with good will but present the risk of making us believe that we have the power of manipulating God.

God is an untranslatable symbol, and undoubtedly remains irreplaceable for very many people. But we ought to be aware that we are dealing with a symbol that is expressed in a word that wishes to say something that, by its very nature, is inexpressible. It is a word we employ in order to understand what is at one and the same time a mystery, a place of freedom, and a kingdom of the infinite.

It is impossible to know God in the sense that we currently give the word *to know*. The only possibility of knowing God is to become God. Access, if we are permitted to call it that, cannot be simply gnoseological. No concept, no idea, can provide that "light, substantial touch" that we neither can know nor reduce to any language. Again the German mystic tells us, repeating a unanimous tradition:

*Je mehr du Gott erkennst, je mehr wirst du bekennen,*
*Dass du weniger ihm, was er ist, kannst kennen.* (V, 41)
The more that you know God, the more you shall confess
That you are able to know less of what he is.

"Let the wise man practice wisdom and not launch into long speeches that are mere empty words," an *Upanishad* says (*Brihadâranyaka Upanishad* IV, 4, 21).

As a kind of synthesis of what human religious traditions teach us, let me offer this: only when we arrive at the triple silence is the experience of God possible. And silence neither means saying nothing nor implies artificially quieting human desires, nor repressing them in any way. The *nirodha* of yoga does not signify an active rejection, just as the Taoist *wu wei* does not recommend laziness, nor the quietude of Molinos the modern *pasotismo.* Neither does Ignatian indifference entail an insensibility to what is human. In the same way, despite abuses, neither should the *ataraxia* of the Epicureans or the *apatheia* of the Stoics be interpreted as an inhuman impassability. Courtesy does not eliminate courage.

Let us turn to the three silences we mentioned earlier:

• *The silence of the intellect* (*mens*), means, the tranquilization of our reason in such a way that ideas no longer dominate our lives. We often act as if human existence were the conclusion of a syllogism that began with first principles. The intelligence maintains silence when it remains respectfully quiet as it confronts the ultimate questions of nothingness that the mind itself undoubtedly presents. To account for this, to be aware that we cannot understand everything, liberates the mind from a weight that is often oppressive. The

Latin liturgy does not speak of *vivere secundum rationem,* "living according to reason," but of a "living in accordance with you" (*secundum te*), through Christ and in the Spirit. This in no way implies that the mind possesses neither rights nor a domain of its own, but only that it is not our ultimate guide, even though it does have the right to veto every irrational action. "It is neither through great instruction nor by means of mental effort nor by the study of Scriptures that we obtain *atman,*" repeats the *Katha Upanishad* (I, 2, 23).

• *The silence of the will,* more difficult to achieve, is not obtained when we have no desire to wish, nor even when we simply fail to. It is achieved when the will no longer makes any sound, when it moves harmoniously in the whole, in order not to speak in the *Tao,* and wishes what ought to be wished, to express it in a paradoxical way. Free will is not individualistic libertinage but the intrinsic dynamism of the Being that is neither determined nor constrained by any external factor. Many schools of spirituality call this purity of heart; others interpret it in terms of an empty heart.

• *The silence of action* refers to the nonviolent action that directs life like an expert helmsman (one of the first meanings of *ophos,* wise one) who is not scrupulous about following the direction of the wind yet knows how to use it. Strong and fruitful action is not measured by the effort or the revolutions it engenders but by the force with which it rules the events of life on the personal, historic, and even cosmic level. The profound meaning, so often misunderstood, of obligations or commandments consists precisely in inspiring us with *karma-yoga,* to adopt an expression from the *Gîtâ.* Your commandments are joyous and liberate the heart, proclaim the Psalms of David.

Let me say this in another way: we experience infinity by means of the intellect, through the knowledge that never reaches its end, as well as through the heart, by means of the love that never totally attains the loved object, and also by the action that never arrives at its fulfillment. That is why silence is required.

The experience of God is, paradoxically, that experience of contingency, which also reveals the tangent between the finite and the infinite. It is an experience that shows that our thought, like our desire and action, never exhausts either its origin or purpose. The self-awareness that we are without beginning or end is, precisely, the experience of Divinity. There are as many psychological paths that lead to this experience as there are people; as many traditional paths as there are religions; as many personal paths as there are religiosities. God belongs neither to the one nor the other, neither to the good nor the wicked: God transcends all our words and faculties. In this experience of empty transcendence, we experience the void; we encounter emptiness and ultimately silence.

This silence is the unique place of freedom. Thought, in fact, is not totally free inasmuch as it is constrained by the principle of noncontradiction. It finds itself constrained by the good, even though such restraint is partial, and even if the will can in fact wander. Action is not pure agitation inasmuch as it moves toward an end that also directs it. Silence alone offers a space for freedom: God is freedom and silence is the "space" needed for experiencing God.

# Propitious Places

In short, every place is propitious for experiencing God if we know how to live in its depths. This ideal is best summarized by commenting on a traditional experience, formulated by a number of sacred or less sacred texts: God is Life. The experience of Life is equivalent to the experience of God. Note that we say experience, *not* reflection about life. To feel oneself alive is not a simple biological act. We speak here not of simple physiological *bios* or the *bios* of a given individual biography. We refer to the *zoè* whose evangelical expression is "eternal Life," an expression we might translate in contemporary terms as "infinite life." We refer not to the instinct for conservation but rather that of feeling life, an instinct proper to human beings precisely insofar as they realize that more than hemoglobin and other physiological ingredients flow in their veins. To feel oneself alive with eternal life does not mean believing oneself immortal in linear time, but rather to experience the reality of "tempiternity," about which so many mystics, poets, and philosophers speak. "Life does not die," the *Vedas* chant, ending the *Upanishads* by saying that God (Brahman) is Life.

We find this kind of experience in Baruch Spinoza's assertion: "We feel ourselves to be immortal and have that experience." He was criticized immediately as a pantheist because he interpreted his experience by means of intellect alone rather than in and through his whole being, which is also bodily. This experience of Life is both subjective and objective genitive: it is the experience of Life itself and our participation in that experience. It is written: "You are Gods," and Scripture cannot "be abolished." Those who have truly "undergone" the experience of God will not fall into the temptation to divinize themselves prematurely—and will find themselves led to the trinitarian intuition.

The reader who has had the patience (which always works for our salvation, Luke 21:19) to read to the end may be surprised at the apparent contradiction between the first pages of this book, in which he or she read that no experience of God was possible, and these last pages, affirming nothing less than the universality of the experience of the divine. That is why my prologue referred to the oxymoron as the non-dualist way of thinking.

It is impossible to experience God as substance and transcendence, and there is no knowledge of the Infinite. But as we have just said, we do have a direct knowledge of our contingency. And precisely in that contingency do we touch (*cum tangere*) the infinite: the Christian expression of this contact is "Incarnation." A different language would tell us that in the experience of *samsâra* we touch *nirvana*. Or, in a manner that is both more poetic and more prosaic: "God is also found in the cooking, mixed in with the soup," as in that *entos* that is the place of God's kingdom (Luke 17:21). We meet God *between* things: *within* their interior and *between* the things and us.

Our contingency is human and divine—at its tangential point. We cannot experience an exclusively immanent God, which we would confuse with a pantheistic identity. Nor can we experience an exclusively transcendent God, which would be contradictory in itself. Instead, we meet God in *relationship*. And, as we have said, we are that point of contact.

# EPILOGUE

Those who have lived the experience of God in one way or another have lost their everyday working identities. All that is left to them is what we might call their profound identity. The experience of God is understood, therefore, as subjective genitive—God's experience. It is not my experience of God. God is not an object—of either faith or experience. It is the experience *of* God that occurs (*experiri*) within me, in which I participate more or less consciously. In this sense, however, the phrase is inexact, since to say that God is part of my experience requires trinitarian precision: it is the Son in the Spirit that constitutes this divine experience.

Our experience of God is the divine self-consciousness in which we participate as we become, in Christian language, part of the "whole Christ"—the *Christus totus.* That is divinization.

On this basis, we say that the man or woman of God, to use a traditional expression, has no identity to differentiate him or her from others. His or her identity identifies them more with the whole of humanity and the entire universe—he or she feels, as Paul says, more Jewish with the Jews, more Greek with the Greeks, more all with all.

One example: the man of God does not consider himself identified or limited, by any given label: Spanish, Indian, academic, philosopher, believer, Catholic, priest, or male. He does not even believe the label of human being or living being is appropriate.

This is the experience of total stripping that the mystics speak about. Those who consider that the label "Christian," for example, separates them from "nonbelievers" confuse their experience of God with their *interpretation* of the experience of God. The one who speaks as an "American," a "scientist," a "male," except on predetermined scientific subjects, leaves aside or confuses the experience of God with *his* or *her* experience of God. Such an experience is not the oceanic, prelogical, or primitive feeling that has frequently been criticized. Rather, *it is the ultimate and universal experience incarnated in the concrete and the particular.* The experience of God cannot be separated from a stroll with a friend, a shared meal, the love that we feel, the idea that we defend, the conversation that unfolds, the pain that we endure—discovering in all this a third dimension of depth, of love, of the infinite—and hence the ineffable. It is a discovery that discloses the value that lies hidden in the deepest and most real of our human acts.

The experience of God is simply the experience of the third dimension—beyond reason, beyond emotion, in faith—of reality, which can show its effect in the profound manner of conducting a human activity, among things or among people, or in concentrating itself in the world of ideas.

In this experience we see, along with classic mystics of many traditions, the dimension of *emptiness* in all things, an emptiness that signifies their uselessness. Utterly real as things are, they nevertheless do reveal something like an emptiness, an absence of something more, if you will. But a something that is not "something in addition," something less, perhaps, than the absolutizing of the thing or the event that we are living through—a something less than the naming (substantiation) of the thing or the event. Because of this *Gelassenheit* or sense of renunciation, an attitude of holy indifference, *asakti* (the act of detaching oneself from things, independence with regard to them), and *wu wei* (nonaction) are judged as fundamental by the mystic, if we may use that name for those who hold their third eye open.

If deprived of the two other dimensions, of course, this vision of the third eye, the eye of faith, is a simple hallucination. The interpretation of this experience, nevertheless, depends on the cultural milieu of the one who interprets it. One of those interpretations gives it the name of *God*—which, in turn, is open to a great variety of meanings.

One clarification is necessary. It is not a question of pantheism or even panentheism—except when we complete our thought by calling it a "panen-psychism" and a "panen-cosmism." Everything is in God just as, analogously, everything is in Consciousness and in the Universe. Each of these three dimensions is interwoven in the other in a way that we have called the cosmotheandric experience, the *perichoresis* or mutual indwelling of the real, the life of the radical Trinity.

The practice of silence is enough to permit "hearing" the music of this third dimension—although that should not be understood to mean that the ability to be silent does not already constitute grace.

In this sense, the experience of God coincides with the fact of seeing God "in" all things—and all things "in" God, if such is the name we wish to give to the Divine.

We understand then that mystics are those whose activity is the most free. They act freely because in all things and events they see an empty "space" that prevents them from being fatalistic and hence makes it possible for them to act with confidence and allows them to believe that what they do is not in vain. They need never judge their action by its immediate effects (cf. the *Gîtâ's* notion of *nais karma karma*).

The experience of God, therefore, distracts us from everyday activities, whatever they may be. Once again, we are not talking about the experience of an object called God, since God is not a thing. We are talking, rather, of an experience of reality in its three constitutive dimensions.

Employing a different language, we would be able to say that it is at once the experience of the thing, of ourselves at the interior of the thing, and of God that embraces both. It is the experience of the cosmotheandric icon of reality at that moment of space and time, from the angle of our personal perspective and in light of our limited and concrete vision.

We have said that the experience of God ought to be understood in the sense of a subjective genitive, that is, as the experience that *God* has, not of a solipsistic self, but of a trinitarian and hence relational and participative Being in which we and all creation enter.

Seen from our side, experienced as starting from us, this experience consists in recovering our original—that is, our natural—state, which in traditional language is imaged as the paradisal state before original sin. That is why we say that the way is redemption, liberation, and fulfillment.

Although it originates in us, this first state is not (the Victorines of the twelfth century said) the one that was given to us and that ought to be recovered and restored.

In this state, we experience what the Greek wisdom cited by Saint Paul says when it recalls that "in it we live, move, and have our being" (Acts 17:28).

This is not the supposed "presence of God," like the *prae-essentia* of a Being whom we are facing, but the more interior, more personal experience, not as if we were moved by another but conscious that the source of our actions and the ultimate subject of our being belongs to that infinite sea that we call God.

We repeat that the experience of a transcendent God is literally impossible: we would soil its spotless transcendence. Such a God does not exist; he is a projection of our mind, the fruit of a monarchical civilization.

The trinitarian God is different; we are inserted into the divine *perichoresis*. I experience myself then as "son"—to repeat a traditional designation that, as Saint Thomas remarked, is only a metaphor. For this reason, Saint Thomas says, John the Evangelist speaks of the Word, not of the Son (*Compendium Theol. 40; Sum. Theol.* q. 27, a.2).

This experience of God is the experience of my profound Self, the paradoxical experience that we are most intimately our own and at the same time superior to ourselves. The necessary condition is to have a pure heart.

The experience of God thus consists in touching the totality of Being with the totality of our own being: to feel in our body, our intellect, and our spirit the whole of reality both *within* us and *outside* us. And paradoxically, it is the experience of contingency: we merely touch the infinite at a point.

The experience of God is the experience of the Mystery that governs our lives from both within and without.

# Illustrations

*All lithographs by Richard Kathmann*

**Richard Kathmann** *earned a BFA from the School of the Art Institute of Chicago and an MFA from New York's Pratt Institute. He taught Observation and Drawing at the State University of New York College at Oneonta and continues to work from his home in the Catskill Mountains of upstate New York. His home studio is a rennovated sap house from his father's farm.*

*February* — Richard Kathmann